MODELING ENVIRONMENTAL POLICY

NATURAL RESOURCE MANAGEMENT AND POLICY

Editors:

Ariel Dinar
Agricultural and Natural Resources Dept.
The World Bank
1818 H Street, NW
Washington, DC 20433

David Zilberman
Dept. of Agricultural and
Resource Economics
Univ. of California, Berkeley
Berkeley, CA 94720

EDITORIAL STATEMENT

There is a growing awareness to the role that natural resources such as water, land, forests and environmental amenities play in our lives. There are many competing uses for natural resources, and society is challenged to manage them for improving social well being . Furthermore, there may be dire consequences to natural resources mismanagement. Renewable resources such as water, land and the environment are linked, and decisions made with regard to one may affect the others. Policy and management of natural resources now require interdisciplinary approach including natural and social sciences to correctly address our society preferences.

This series provides a collection of works containing most recent findings on economics, management and policy of renewable biological resources such as water, land, crop protection, sustainable agriculture, technology, and environmental health. It incorporates modern thinking and techniques of economics and management. Books in this series will incorporate knowledge and models of natural phenomena with economics and managerial decision frameworks to assess alternative options for managing natural resources and environment.

Environment is a complex ecosystem which needs to be appropriately addressed in policy evaluation. The Martin-McDonald book adds to our understanding of this complexity by combining approaches from various disciplines. The book demonstrates the importance of using results obtained by models from one discipline as inputs to models of another discipline to generate an integrated information system necessary for policy analysis.

The Series Editors

Recently Published Books in the Series

Schmitz, A., Moulton, K., Buckwell, A. and Davidova, S.:
Privatization of Agriculture in New Market Economies: Lessons from Bulgaria
Pingali, P. and Roger, P.:
Impact of Pesticides on Farmer Health and the Rice Environment
Bovenberg, L. and Cnossen, S.:
Public Economics and the Environment in an Imperfect World

MODELING ENVIRONMENTAL POLICY

edited by

Wade E. Martin
Colorado School of Mines

Lisa A. McDonald
Hazen and Sawyer, P.C.

Kluwer Academic Publishers
Boston/Dordrecht/London

Distributors for North America:
Kluwer Academic Publishers
101 Philip Drive
Assinippi Park
Norwell, Massachusetts 02061 USA

Distributors for all other countries:
Kluwer Academic Publishers Group
Distribution Centre
Post Office Box 322
3300 AH Dordrecht, THE NETHERLANDS

Library of Congress Cataloging-in-Publication Data
Modeling environmental policy / edited by Wade E. Martin, Lisa A.
  McDonald.
        p.   cm. -- (Natural resource management and policy)
    Includes index.
    ISBN 0-7923-9855-6
    1. Environmental policy--United States--Mathematical models.
    2. Pollution--United States--Decision making--Mathematical models.
    I. Martin, Wade E.   II. McDonald, Lisa A.   III. Series.
    GE180.M64   1997
    363.7'00973--dc21   93-51423
                                                              CIP

Printed on acid-free paper.

Printed in the United States of America

Table of Contents

Table of Contents   v

Contributing Authors   vii

1   *Wade E. Martin & Lisa A. McDonald*   1
    Modeling Environmental Policy: An Introduction

2   *Aziz Bouzaher & Jason Shogren*   7
    Modeling Nonpoint Source Pollution in an Integrated System

3   *David G. Abler & James S. Shortle*   43
    Modeling Environmental & Trade Policy Linkages: The Case of EU and US Agriculture

4   *Philip F. Roan & Wade E. Martin*   77
    Modeling Ecosystem Constraints in the Clean Water Act: A Case Study in Clearwater National Forest

5   *Timothy J. Considine, Graham A. Davis & Donita Marakovits*   103
    Costs & Benefits of Coke Oven Emission Controls

6   *Alain Haurie & Richard Loulou*   123
    Modeling Equilibria and Risk Under Global Environmental Constraints

7   *Imma J. Curiel, Jerzy A. Filar & Radoslaw Zapert*   161
       Relative Contribution of the Enhanced
       Greenhouse Effect on the Coastal Changes
       in Louisiana

8   *Kathleen A. Miller*   185
       The Use of Mathematical Models in
       Policy Evaluation: Comments

Index   199

Contributing Authors

David G. Abler, Associate Professor of Agricultural Economics, Department of Agricultural Economics, The Pennsylvania State University, University Park, Pennsylvania 16802.

Aziz Bouzaher, Senior Economist, The World Bank, 1818 H Street, N.W., Washington D.C. 20433.

Timothy J. Considine, Associate Professor, Department of Energy, Environmental, and Mineral Economics, The Pennsylvania State University, University Park, Pennsylvania 16802.

Imma J. Curiel, Associate Professor, Department of Mathematics and Statistics, University of Maryland-Baltimore County, Baltimore, Maryland.

Graham A. Davis, Assistant Professor of Mineral Economics, Division of Economics and Business, Colorado School of Mines, Golden, Colorado 80401-1887

Jerzy A. Filar, Professor of Mathematics and Statistics & Director, Center for Industrial & Applied Mathematics, University of South Australia, The Levels SA 5095, Australia.

Alain Haurie, Professor of Operations Research, Department of Management Studies, University of Geneva, Geneva, Switzerland.

Richard Loulou, Professor of Quantitative Methods, Faculty of Management, McGill University, Montreal, Quebec, Canada.

Donita Marakovits, Department of Energy, Environmental and Mineral Economics, The Pennsylvania State University, University Park, Pennsylvania 16802.

Wade E. Martin, Associate Professor & Director, Environmental Policy Center, Division of Economics & Business, Colorado School of Mines, Golden, Colorado 80401-1887.

Lisa A. McDonald, Economist, Hazen & Sawyer, P.C., 4000 Hollywood Boulevard, Seventh Floor, North Tower, Hollywood, Florida 33021.

Kathleen A. Miller, Scientist III, Environmental and Societal Impacts Group, National Center for Atmospheric Research, P.O. Box 3000, Boulder, Colorado 80307.

Philip F. Roan, Quantitative Analyst, Koch Supply and Trading Company, P.O. Box 2256, Wichita, Kansas 67201.

Jason Shogren, Thomas Stroock Distinguished Professor of Natural Resource Conservation and Management, Department of Economics & Finance, University of Wyoming, Laramie, Wyoming 82071.

James S. Shortle, Professor of Agricultural Economics, Department of Agricultural Economics, The Pennsylvania State University, University Park, Pennsylvania 16802.

Radoslaw Zapert, Associate, Coopers & Lybrand, L.L.P., 1301 Avenue of the Americas, New York, New York 10019-6013.

Chapter 1
Modeling Environmental Policy:
An Introduction

Wade E. Martin
Lisa A. McDonald

The physical complexity of environmental systems or ecosystems has long been recognized. It is often argued that policy analysts do not sufficiently consider this complexity in their evaluation of policy options for environmental regulations. In a world of perfect information and efficient markets the need for environmental policies would not exist since all scarce resources, including the environment, would be allocated based upon their scarcity value. However, such is not the case and throughout the world political institutions are faced with the task of correcting market failures associated with the use of the environment. To develop the appropriate policy prescription for the various types of pollution requires the input of a vast array of expertise. Disciplines such as engineering, chemistry, physics, sociology, psychology, and economics to name just a few are critical to effective and efficient development of environmental regulations.

An important consideration in developing environmental policy is that *all* of the various disciplines must be able to communicate with each other. A particular endpoint for one discipline is often the starting point, or initial conditions, for another discipline. For example, when regulating a toxic substance such as asbestos fibers, the endpoint of the epidemiologist regarding the exposure level is a critical input into an economist's benefit-cost analysis of a particular policy option to control the toxic substance. Each of the disciplines involved must have a common language. Most frequently, this common language is *mathematics*. The dose-response models of epidemiologists or the pollution transport models of geochemists can be designed to provide the endpoints necessary as inputs into policy models. The papers in this volume demonstrate the link between the physical models of the environment and the policy analysis in support of policy making.

The use of mathematics as a common language requires that each discipline have the necessary understanding of the mathematical tools required for modeling the particular policy issue. The extent of this understanding does not have to include an in-depth understanding of the paradigm appropriate for a discipline, however, it does require an understanding of the methodology used to generate the endpoints to design effective environmental policy. The papers in this volume demonstrate the importance of taking the endpoints from the models of one discipline and using them as inputs in the models of other disciplines. In some cases, the models are directly linked to each other to generate an integrated system for policy modeling.

Mathematically based policy models can be constructed in two ways, as qualitative models and as quantitative models. Qualitative models provide insight into the direction of change that a particular policy will induce without providing information as to the magnitude of that change. Quantitative models provide information not only on the direction of the change but also on the magnitude of the change. Many policy makers have been hesitant to use mathematical models in the decision making process because of the perceived lack of relevance of the results. This has often been the case when using qualitative models. Each of the chapters in this volume, however, addresses an environmental policy issue using a quantitative modeling approach. The efforts of the authors demonstrate that important and useful numerical results can be obtained that will assist in the decision making process for policy makers.

The papers in this volume address three general areas of environmental policy. These are 1) non-point source pollution in the agriculture sector; 2) pollution generated in the extractive industries; and 3) transboundary pollutants from burning fossil fuels. A concluding chapter that discusses the modeling efforts and the use of mathematical models in general is then presented.

Non-point Source Pollution

The agricultural sector of the economy has come under much scrutney regarding the release of non-point source pollutants associated with the application of fertilizers. Chapters 2 and 3 by Bouzaher & Shogren and Abler & Shortle, respectively present models that consider the impacts of various policy options on the release of such pollutants. Bouzaher & Shogren focus on the development of an integrated agri-ecological economic system to examine the impact of environmental policies. Abler & Shortle model the linkages between the environment and trade policies in the United States and the European Community. An analysis of environmental and trade linkages in these two economies is critical due to the potential impact on the negotiations over the General Agreement on Tariffs and Trade (GATT).

Bouzaher & Shogren focus on three issues. First, the effect of unilateral versus coordinated policy. The primary focus here is on the often conflicting polices of the United States Department of Agriculture (USDA) and the U.S. Environmental Protection Agency (EPA). Second, the authors consider the impact on input substitution from various environmental policies. Such considerations are important to fully understand the impact that a given environmental policy will have on pollutant concentrations or emissions. The third issue is a discussion of metamodels to integrate a system of models. Such an approach is important in linking the models from various disciplines, in this case ecology and economics. These three issues are analyzed in the context of the Comprehensive Environmental Economic Policy Evaluation System (CEEPES). The policy scenarios analyzed are a ban on atrazine and on all triazines.

The work of Abler & Shortle focuses on the importance of linking environmental and trade policy to non-point source water pollution impacts. These authors analyze the agricultural policy reform proposals in the U.S. and the E.C. The timeliness of the analysis is evident given the current discussions in both the U.S. and the E.C. regarding agricultural policy reform. The discussions in the U.S. focus on cutting price supports and reforming supply controls. Whereas, the E.C. has proposed extensive reforms to the Common Agricultural Policy (CAP). The impact on the environment of each of these proposals needs to be modeled. Abler & Shortle develop their analysis based upon a partial equilibrium simulation of agriculture in the U.S., the E.C. and the rest of the world. The policy scenarios considered are CAP reforms in the E.C., price support cuts in the U.S. and restrictions on fertilizers and agricultural chemicals in the E.C. Three commodities common to both the U.S. and the E.C. are considered: wheat, coarse grains and soybeans.

Extractive Industries

Chapters 4 and 5 consider the impact of environmental policies on the extractive industries. Chapter 4 by Roan & Martin focus on water quality issues at the mine site, whereas, chapter 5 by Considine, Davis & Marakovits analyze the regulation of fugitive air emissions from coke ovens. These two chapters provide insight into environmental regulations in the extractive industries at both the mine site and the processing sector. The tools and modeling techniques to consider such impacts frequently differ.

Roan & Martin consider the impact of water quality regulations under the Clean Water Act on the optimal rate of extraction of ore and the optimal level of reclamation activity. The effect of regulations on metal concentrations, extraction and reclamation is then used to determine the impact on mine profitability and ore grade. The modeling techniques used by the authors is optimal control theory. Such a technique permits the consideration of the dynamics of the regulatory effects. Empirical results are obtained using linear cost functions that have been estimated by the U.S. Bureau of Mines for a typical open-pit mine. The model extends the traditional mine model by incorporating a transition equation that models the ecosystem constraint imposed by the environmental policy on water quality standards for stream metal concentrations.

Considine, *et al.* analyze the impact of Title III of the Clean Air Act Amendments requiring the EPA to establish emission standards for coke oven batteries. The authors use an integrated engineering-economics model of the steel production process. This model is a linear programming model that minimizes costs based upon a number of market and non-market constraints. The authors consider two regulatory prescriptions that are based upon Title III. First, the EPA must issue emission control standards based upon a Maximum Achievable Control Technology (MACT) by December 31, 1995. Second, another set of standards are to be implemented by January 1, 1998 based upon the Lowest Achievable Emission Rate (LAER). Considine, *et al.* consider five technological options for compliance with the MACT and LAER regulations. These are: using sodium silicate luting compounds to plug leaks; retrofitting existing ovens; totally rebuilding coke ovens; adopting new coke oven technologies; or adopting new coke-saving production technologies. Another alternative discussed is importing coke or other down-stream products to avoid the production emissions altogether. The results of the modeling effort are used in a stochastic benefit-cost analysis of the proposed regulations.

Transboundary Pollutants

Haurie & Loulou and Curiel, Filar & Zapert present models of transboundary pollutants that have been the focus of much debate in both the academic literature and the general press. Burning fossil fuel has been at the center of one of the most widely debated sources of pollution. The two primary environmental issues that have been associated with the use of fossil fuel are acid deposition and global climate change. Haurie & Loulou address the modeling of the first issue and Curiel, *et al.* the second.

In chapter 6 Haurie & Loulou consider the contribution of optimization techniques to analyzing the interrelations between the economy, energy and the global environment. The authors argue that a mathematical programming framework provides the necessary foundation to meet three important criteria in a modeling effort. These criteria are: presentation of a sufficiently detailed representation of techno-economic options; a coherent representation of the economic processes; and tractability of simulations or scenarios. These three criteria are discussed in the framework of three approaches to modeling the interactions between the economy, energy and the environment. The three approaches are: the market equilibrium (supply/demand) paradigm; cooperative and noncooperative game theory; and uncertainty models. The first approach applies the MARKAL (MARKet ALlocation) model to the case of emissions analysis in Quebec and Ontario. Second, the authors apply game theory to the energy-environment-economy modeling in the New England-Quebec-Ontario area. Finally, a dynamic stochastic programming approach is detailed for analysis of risk management decisions.

Curiel, *et al.* develop a model that uses the endpoints (output) of a climate change model as an input into a local model of the Louisiana coastline to determine the impact of various climate change scenarios. The authors use the IMAGE model developed in the Netherlands and combine it with the SEAL model which the authors developed. This chapter also uses the optimal control technique to model the dynamics of the environment. An interesting result of linking the IMAGE model to the SEAL model is the ability to analyze the impact of the various scenarios of IMAGE as well as the scenarios from the SEAL model.

The final chapter by Miller comments on the techniques used by each of the other papers in the volume as well as general insights into the use of mathematical models for policy analysis. The comments by Miller provide an interesting bases for evaluating the desirability of using mathematics as the common language in policy analysis debates.

Chapter 2
Modeling Nonpoint Source Pollution
in an Integrated System

Aziz Bouzaher
Jason Shogren

Introduction

Nonpoint source pollution from the agricultural sector is forcing regulators to rethink national environmental and agricultural policy. Nonpoint sources include the handling and disposal of animal wastes, application of chemical fertilizers to cropland, soil erosion, and sedimentation from cultural practices, and the use of pesticides in crop production. New policy strategies that are explicitly coordinated between the United States Department of Agriculture (USDA) and the Environmental Protection Agency (EPA) may well be necessary to efficiently reduce human and wildlife risk at minimal impact on agricultural producers. But evaluating these proposed strategies will require both economic and environmental indicators of success. These indicators must be estimated in a timely fashion before policies are finalized. Consequently, there has been increased attention on constructing an integrated agri-ecological economic modeling system that can simulate the potential tradeoffs of new policy strategies.

This paper addresses three key issues in modeling nonpoint source pollution in an integrated agri-ecological economic system. First, we examine the issue of unilateral versus coordinated policy. The USDA and the EPA have long operated in their own spheres where the efforts to integrate policy have been more lip service than anything else. Second, we consider the issue of input substitution in crop production. By focusing on alternative weed control strategies, we illustrate the necessity of defining a detailed set of input substitutes. Without a detailed understanding of how producers will substitute inputs given a proposed policy, we will misspecify the consequences of the policy. Third, we describe how metamodels can be used to effectively integrate the system. Metamodels are statistical response functions that summarize the key characteristics of economic and environmental models, thereby making the modeling system more flexible and responsive to new policy strategies.

We define these issues within the context of the Comprehensive Environmental Economic Policy Evaluation System (CEEPES). CEEPES is an integrated system designed to evaluate systematically alternative policy strategies, both coordinated or unilateral. We illustrate the importance of policy integration, input substitution, and metamodeling by estimating the economic and environmental impacts of a ban on atrazine and on all triazines—atrazine, bladex, and princep. Our preliminary results suggest that an atrazine ban decreases agricultural net returns, while increasing the exposure values of substitute herbicides. Overall, the benefits of an atrazine ban are questionable.

Agri-ecological Economic Policy

The EPA is responsible for maintaining the integrity of water quality in the United States. While there is no evidence of significant widespread risks from pesticide use, monitoring by the United States Geological Survey and by state governments suggests water quality has been impaired in certain areas. Since water contamination, especially groundwater, could well be irreversible, the EPA seeks to develop a preventive strategy. Nevertheless, the Agency's current program focuses on ex ante preventive strategies rather than an ex post curative remedies. If a pesticide has or is expected to exceed reference risk levels, the EPA expects either the state authority to take strong actions to stop further contamination or it will step in with restrictions at the federal level (USEPA, 1991).

One action to reduce contamination is to cancel the use of pesticides expected to exceed reference risk levels. Under the authority of the Federal Insecticide, Fungicide, and Rodenticide Act (FIFRA) and the Federal Food, Drug, and Cosmetic Act (FFDCA), the EPA can regulate the use of a pesticide. If a pesticide is suspected of posing unreasonable adverse effects to humans or the environment, the EPA can initiate a Special Review. Based on the EPA's risk assessment and rebuttal testimony by the registrant, the EPA's regulatory options fall into three categories:

•continued registration with no changes;
•modifications such as restricted use, timing, and applications; and
•cancellations or suspensions.

Of course, the EPA is not alone, the United States Department of Agriculture (USDA) has the biggest impact on the agricultural sector with its set of commodity programs. The forerunner to current USDA policy started in the New Deal era of the 1930s. With the objectives of stabilizing output supply, farm income, and price, an intricate set of program incentives have evolved over the past fifty years for most major commodities.

While soil erosion has always been a concern, the USDA's attention to general environmental issues, such as water quality, is more recent. The Food Security Act of 1985 and the Food, Agricultural, Conservation, and Trade Act of 1990 signaled the change. The Acts directly tied program participation to environmental quality. The cross-compliance measures of swampbuster, sodbuster, and conservation compliance were created to restrict the environmental damages associated with introducing new land into production.

The farmer now serves two masters—the USDA and the EPA. Both agencies have unique incentive systems that will impact the behavior of profit maximizing producers. The EPA can unilaterally restrict or ban selected agri-chemicals, while the USDA can unilaterally set price subsidies to output such that intensive agri-chemical use is promoted. The need to coordinate and integrate agricultural and environmental policy seems obvious. Unilateral acts generally expend valuable resource at no gain in environmental quality (Shogren & Crocker, 1991).

Modeling nonpoint source pollution requires identification of the current layers of unilateral policies and possible new coordinated policy options. In fact, the integrated modeling system can be used to determine which, if any, of the new coordinated policy options are attractive to both economic and environmental concerns. The modeling system can act as a focal point around which the debate can focus. The ex ante best and the worst ideas can be systemically explored. One question the system can address is whether it is more efficient to readjust or patch up the current layer of policies or to scrap the system and start anew.

An example of an integrated policy would be to evaluate the trade-offs between the EPA's restrictions on chemical use and the USDA's allowance for increased flexibility in crop production decisions. Flexibility would allow the producer to plant crops other than the program crop without losing access to the program payments. An integrated modeling system could evaluate the risks and benefits of allowing more flexibility with less restrictions. As the producer gains flexibility, chemical restrictions become less important. The flexibility-restriction trade-off is just one example. The argument can be applied more generally.

Input Substitution

Understanding input substitution is critical. Alternative policy strategies will provide different incentives to agricultural producers that may cause them to change their input sets. Unless there is the unlikely policy of, say a complete ban on all pesticides, we need to know how producers will substitute inputs to maximize their returns. It may well be that the producer has a vast set of nearly perfect substitutes to a targeted chemical such that a ban will have trivial economic impacts at no gain in environmental quality. The other side is that the input set is so unique that any policy restriction will cause great economic damages.

We illustrate an approach to model input substitution for weed control in corn and sorghum production. The Weather Impact Simulation on Herbicide (WISH) was developed to simulate the effects of policy on trade-offs in weed control management. The WISH model simulates over 300 alternative weed control strategies for corn and over 90 strategies for sorghum. All weed control strategies are aimed at full control (i.e., under ideal weather conditions, and if applied properly, would result in virtually no yield loss). Clearly, under ideal conditions, cost would be the basis for choosing a weed control strategy. In addition, it is important to note that when we talk about herbicide substitutes, we mean substitutes within a complete feasible strategy, and not a one-to-one chemical substitute. Bouzaher *et al.* (1992) describe the WISH model in detail. We briefly sketch the basic structure below with Figure 2-1 illustrating the major steps simulated by WISH.

We assume farmers trade expected pest-damage for expected application cost when deciding to adopt a pest control strategy. Often weather conditions can be too wet for farmers to get into the field to apply herbicides or cultivate, or weather conditions can be too dry during the critical times for herbicides to be effective, implying additional application cost or yield losses or both. Risk is defined in WISH as the probability a given herbicide strategy is ineffective. An environmental policy such as a herbicide ban or a modification of application technology will change the set of efficient weed control strategies.

Based on herbicide timing of application and effectiveness, mode of application, targeted weeds, and observed farming practices, we construct a herbicide decision tree to represent the average farmer's most likely management approach to pest control. We assume farmers have a main strategy for weed control and a back-up strategy in case of a failure of the main strategy. All this information is combined to define:

(1) The structure of a herbicide strategy, which is assumed to be made up of a primary herbicide treatment (to be applied on an early pre-plant, pre-emergence, or even post-emergence basis), and a secondary herbicide treatment (mainly post-emergence) which would be applied only if the

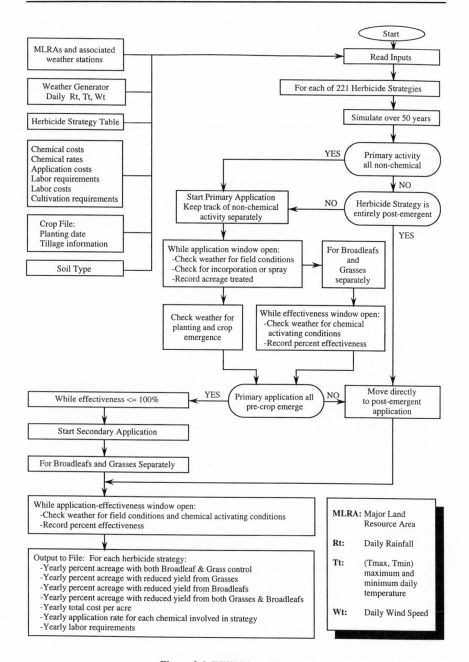

Figure 2-1 WISH Macro Flowchart

primary substrategy fails for reasons mainly related to weather. Note that a strategy rests on the key assumption that, under "normal" weather conditions,it will achieve complete weed control (both grasses and broadleafs). Finally, a herbicide strategy structure is completed by specifying a "time window of application" and a "time window of effectiveness" for each of its primary and secondary components, and for each weed group.

(2) The list of all feasible herbicide strategies. The list is established by tillage practice and by timing of application and scope of control of each herbicide in the strategy. The list is also built with the policy specifications in mind, thereby distinguishing between such strategies as using atrazine alone, at rates lower or higher than 1.5 pounds, strategies using triazine substitutes for atrazine (bladex and princep), and strategies using nontriazines, in various combinations. These feasible strategies are individually simulated to determine their yearly cost, labor requirements, application rates, and percent effectiveness for each weed group and each of two soil texture characteristics, sand and clay.

WISH reads the herbicide strategy table and a weather file which contains daily average information on temperature, rainfall, and wind. For each herbicide strategy over a period of 50 years of weather history, starting with the primary application, the model considers rainfall and wind and records the percentage of acres treated during the window of application; it also records the application rate and cost for each chemical used, and any cultivation requirements. Time advances and weather conditions are checked during the window of effectiveness. An indicator variable cumulatively records the percentage effectiveness of the primary strategy for each weed group. If this variable is less than one, the secondary application is triggered and the same information is recorded. It is important to note that the main objective of this simulation is to capture the effect of those special years (too dry or too wet) where a farmer may have to apply herbicide more than once and still sustain some yield loss (in addition to higher cost), or does not have time to apply herbicide and sustain a major yield loss. The model assumes that three days are enough for a farmer to treat all his acres and fixed planting dates for corn (May 10) and sorghum (June 1), and provides for handling of special cases where strategies involve split applications (part pre-emerge and part post-emerge) or entirely post-emerge applications.

The impact of weed competition on crop yields was simulated using ALMANAC--Agricultural Land Management Alternatives with Numerical Assessment Criteria (Jones and O'Toole, 1986). ALMANAC is a process model that simulates crop growth, weed competition, and the interactions of management factors, for a variety of soil properties and climatic conditions.

Consequently, weed competition models need to be used in conjunction with other models, like WISH, capable of predicting the effectiveness (measured by cost and risk) of various weed control strategies. Farmers typically use weed control strategies aimed at achieving full control, and these strategies either work or fail when environmental conditions either prevent the application of herbicide or impair its effectiveness. These unfavorable conditions are usually associated with extremes in weather conditions, too dry or too wet. WISH and ALMANAC are interfaced to produce, for each weed control strategy, distributions of cost, labor use, application rate (for each chemical in the strategy), and yield loss; the means of the distribution are then used in the economic optimization model.

Metamodels and System Integration

If one is interested in determining the ecological and economic impacts of national policy, then rerunning simulation models of fundamental processes every time a new policy is considered becomes prohibitively expensive (see Cabe *et al.*, 1991). A policy scenario within the integrated system of models is a mutually consistent combination of policy restrictions. If the policy space (S), the parameter space (P), and the simulation period space (T) are moderately large, then a complete policy analysis may require system evaluations at every point (p,s,t) in the Cartessian product set {PxSxT}. In addition, if sensitivity analysis about key parameters is required, then even more evaluations will be necessary.

In practice, these evaluations are extremely cumbersome, expensive, or impractical without some means of reducing the burden of computation. Especially in unified ecological economic systems, ease of computation must be accomplished for both timely integration of diverse process models and integration of outcomes over a distribution of diverse input vectors. The ability to easily evaluate the outcome of a simulation model every time is a requirement for integration with the next model in the ecological economic chain; the integrated system should be linked as closely as model structures allow.

Integrating outcomes over a distribution of inputs requires producing a simulated outcome for any set of inputs and would transfer every observation in a distribution of input vectors to the desired outcome measure, weighted appropriately, and added into the sum. Each time the model directly estimates the outcome for specified input values, something on the order of a few million calculations may be required. In practice, such methods are rarely feasible, either due to limitations of computation time, or because of some manual operations required to transform one model's output into a form suitable for the next model's input.

Metamodeling through response functions provides an analytical tool to address both of these difficulties. A metamodel is a statistical model of the actual simulation model. The concept of a metamodel corresponds to a hierarchical modeling approach whereby we proceed from a complex and "messy" real phenomenon to a well structured simulation model and then to modeling the relationship between inputs and outputs of the simulation model itself.

Consider how metamodeling works with the ALMANAC model that explains process of weed competition upon crop yield, and how the process can improve our understanding of the loading effect of different agrichemical strategies on the environment. The simulation model is built by physical scientists and simulates the processes describing the growth of individual plants and their competition for important resources like water, nutrients, and light, all this within specific management, climatic, and environmental conditions. The complexity of the model stems, in part, from the large number of parameters that require calibration and the time and cost needed to generate information for a large number of locations.

We note that these models were initially designed as research tools to study very small scale phenomena (growth processes of individual plants or competition between two plants within a square meter) and, when projected at the regional level, present challenging aggregation and computational problems. The use of a metamodel in this case is much more than a simplifying step, as would be the case for a conventional simulation model. A key feature of the methodology is to statistically sample from micro data to build parametric forms for prediction at the macro level; that is, while the individual samples are based on very small area features, the metamodel is used to first integrate and then distribute these features over very large areas. Sampling is carried out after a testing phase aimed essentially at factor screening and parameter selection.

The full experimental design phase identifies the exogenous variable to be sampled and the response variables to be recorded; it also determines the minimum number of simulation replications given time or budget constraints or both. Finally, the last step consists in building statistical response functions for the variables of interest (e.g., crop yield, plant biomass, chemical concentration). This step is similar to any model building step with its many facets including diagnostics, variable selection, model specification, estimation, residual analysis, and hypothesis testing, but it differs in one fundamental respect in that the metamodel summarizes relationships but not causality. This metamodeling approach was used to estimate yearly yield loss response functions for corn, corn silage, sorghum and sorghum silage. Significant parameters in these functions are: slope, percent sand, percent clay, bulk density, organic water, ph, weed, weed density, and weather station.

Metamodels are important to estimate environmental consequences. The Fate and Transport models use information on agricultural activity in each geographic unit to produce damage-relevant concentration measures for (a) each damage category, (b) the geographic unit where the chemical was applied, and (c) other geographic units which may be affected by pollutant transport. For example, given an agricultural activity in a rural central Corn Belt geographic unit, the fate and transport component estimates shallow groundwater concentrations relevant to domestic wells and surface water concentrations in the area. The component transforms a vector describing agricultural activity in all geographic units into a vector of ambient concentration measures for each medium in all geographic units. The concentration measures can include expected values, information on the probabilities of various concentrations, or the distributions of concentrations over time and space. Outcomes of greatest interest are 24 hour peak concentrations for acute toxicity and annual average concentrations for long term exposure.

The core of the Fate and Transport system is the Risk of the Unsaturated/Saturated Transport and Transformation of Chemical Concentrations (RUSTIC) model (Dean et al., 1989). RUSTIC is an extension of the Pesticide Root Zone Model (PRZM), which was developed to simulate one-dimensional pesticide transport only through the soil root zone (Carsel et al., 1984). Two additional models, VADOFT and SAFTMOD, are linked to PRZM to simulate pesticide movement in the variably saturated vadose zone and saturated zone. PRZM can be linked directly to SAFTMOD if the simple water balance routine used in PRZM is adequate for the conditions being simulated.

Based on our metamodeling approach, chemical concentration response functions were estimated at 1.2m (the root zone), 15m, and edge of field runoff for both corn and sorghum. The 15m depth corresponds to that used in monitoring studies. Both average and peak chemical concentrations in surface and groundwater are a function of chemical parameters (e.g., Henry's constant, organic carbon partitionary coefficient (KOC), decay rate), soil parameters (e.g., percent sand, organic matter, bulk density, soil depth, water retention capacity), management parameters (e.g., tillage, timing of application), and weather station (see Bouzaher et al., 1994).

We now briefly consider model integration. Integration refers to the process of linking the various components of CEEPES into a unified model for the purpose of conducting policy simulations, and to the aggregation of the results into regional indicators of risks and benefits. Note that metamodels play a major role in integration—they are a parametric representation of physical models linked through their inputs and outputs. The linkages in CEEPES connect the following: (1) ALMANAC, WISH, and RAMS, (2) RAMS and RUSTIC, (3) WISH and RUSTIC, (4) RUSTIC and STREAM, and (5) RUSTIC and the atmospheric models PAL and BLAYER (see figure 2-2). We illustrate the choice of agricultural practices under alternative policies by combining WISH with the Resource Adjustable Modeling System (RAMS) (see Bouzaher et al., 1991). RAMS is a regional, short-term, static profit maximizing, linear programming (LP) model of agricultural production, defined at the producing area (PA) level. The goal of the RAMS model is to estimate the economic impact of alternative agricultural and environmental policies in terms of acreage planted, rotation, tillage practice, chemical regime, yield, and cost of production for each producing area in the study area.

The crucial linkages are those between the agricultural decision component and the physical process models. The process of weed competition was incorporated into RAMS through WISH, the core of the weed control management sector. Figure 2-3 shows the interface between RAMS and RUSTIC. The interfaces translate data on production, technology, and chemical use from RAMS into input required by the RUSTIC metamodels. A key factor underlying this operation is the chemical application rate. Figures 2-4 and 2-5 summarize the integrated system. First, for each policy scenario and PA, chemical concentrations and exposure values are computed by crop, chemical, tillage, and environmental media for each soil series in the PA. Aggregation of concentrations and exposure values can then be performed (a) geographically, by county, PA, State, or USDA-region level, (b) across chemicals, (c) across environmental media, and (d) across

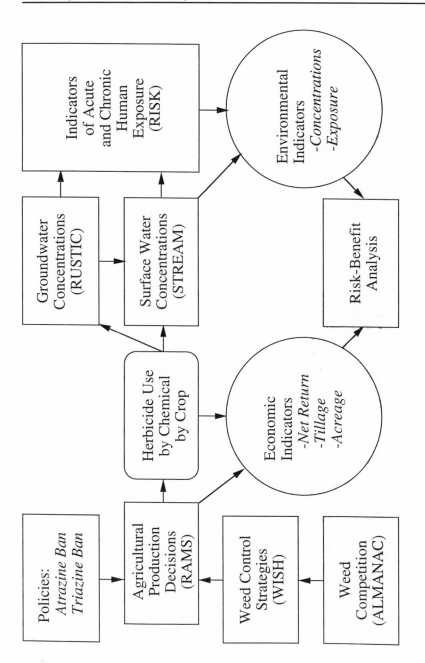

Figure 2-2 Experimental Design of CEEPES for Water Quality

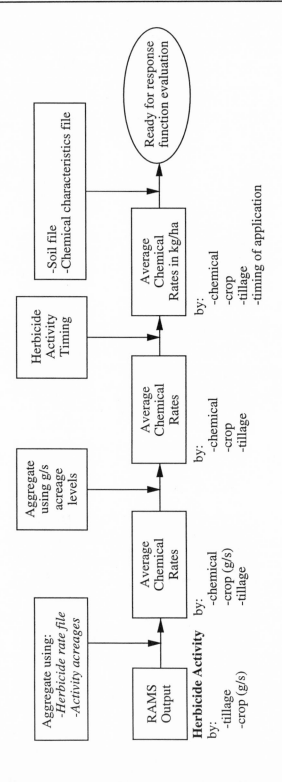

Figure 2-3 RAMS/RUSTIC Interface

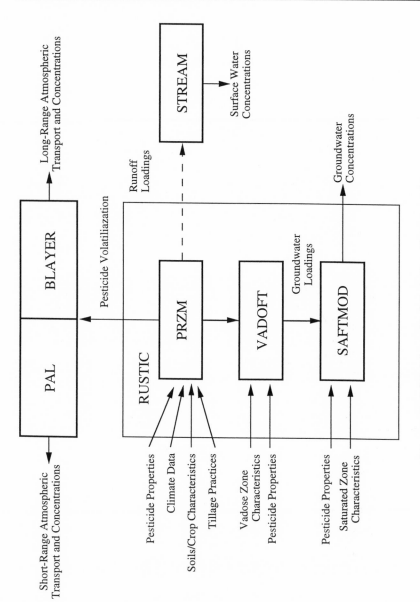

Figure 2-4 Multi-media Modeling Framework

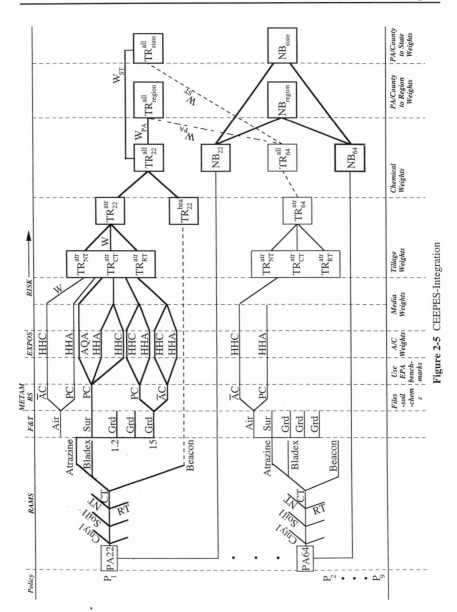

Figure 2-5 CEEPES-Integration

Legend for Figure 2-5

P_1 : $1 = 1. \ldots .g$: policy scenario l

Pa_{xx} :   Producing area xx

Cntyx: County x

Soilx: Soil x

NT: No tillage

CT: Conventional tillage

RT: Ridge tillage

F&T: Fate and transport

Air: Air transport

Sur: Surface water

Grd: Ground Water

METAM: Metamodels

C: Average concentration

PC: Peak concentration

EXPOS: Exposures

HHC: Human health chronic

HHA: Human health acute

AQA: Aquatic acute

W :   Weighting scheme for environmental media

TR_{NT}^{atr} :   Total risk from atrazine under no till production systems

TR_{22}^{atr} :   Total risk from atrazine in producing area 22

TR_{22}^{bea} :   Total risk from beacon in producing area 22

TR_{22}^{all} :   Total risk from all chemicals in producing area 22

NB_{22} :   Net benefit in producing area 22

W_{PA} :   Weighting scheme from producing area to USDA region

TR_{region}^{all} :   Total risk from all chemicals in USDA region

W_{ST} :   Weighting scheme from producing area to state

TR_{state}^{all} :   Total risk from all chemicals in state

NB_{state} :   Net benefit in State

technologies. Given the appropriate weights, any combination of the above aggregations can be obtained and compared to the economic benefits of the policy scenario under consideration.

The final step of integration is to transform chemical concentrations into a common unit that will allow comparisons of policy and potential for risk. The peak and average chemical concentration levels found in surface and groundwater can be transformed into a unitless measure of exposure. Pesticide specific benchmarks for health and environmental effects are used to weight the relative importance of changes in exposure levels without more detailed assessment. The ratios derived from such benchmarks do not serve as absolute indicators of adverse impacts. Using the benchmark concentrations for human toxicity derived by EPA procedures we calculate the toxicity-weighted exposure level by chemical.

$$Toxicity-Weighted\ Exposure\ =\ \frac{predicted\ concentration}{EPA\ Benchmark\ Concentration}$$

for both peak and average levels. The exposure value acts to normalize the concentrations allowing us to compare risks across chemicals and across policies. A chemical concentration presents a greater risk the larger the exposure value. Note that if the exposure values exceeds unity, the concentration has exceeded the benchmark. But the necessity of less than perfect model calibration implies that the greater reliance should be placed on relative differences between risk levels than on absolute levels. The further from unity the greater the potential risk. An exposure level below unity implies concentration levels are below the EPA's benchmark dose values. Table 2-1 presents the EPA dose response values for the seventeen chemicals we considered in our analysis.

An Application of the CEEPES System

We summarize the economic and environmental indicators of our baseline, atrazine ban, and triazine ban runs by the three main regions--Corn Belt, Lake States, and Northern Plains. The economic indicators include net return-- revenue minus costs--changes in crop production acreage both overall and by tillage, changes in corn and sorghum acreage by tillage, and changes in herbicide application on corn and sorghum. The environmental indicators include average and peak concentrations by chemical for groundwater at 1.2m and 15m, and peak concentrations for surface water. These concentrations are also converted into both

Table 2-1
EPA Toxicity Benchmarks for Humans
Acute and Chronic

Herbicide		Water Exposures	
Chemical	Trade Name	Acute	Chronic
Atrazine	AAtrex	100 ppb	3 ppb
Alachlor	Lasso	100 ppb	2 ppb[a]
Bentazon	Basagran	25 ppb	20 ppb
Bromoxynil	Buctril	700 ppb[b]	140 ppb[a]
Butylate	Sutan	2.4 ppm	50 ppb
Cyanazine	Bladex	100 ppb	8 ppb
Dioamba	Banvel	300 ppb	9 ppb
EPTC	Eradicane	875 ppb[b]	175 ppb[b]
Glyphosate	Round-up	20 ppm	700 ppb
Metolachlor	Dual	100 ppb	100 ppb
Paraquat	Gramaxine	100 ppb	30 ppb
Pendimethalin	Prowl	1.4 ppm[b]	0.3 ppm[b]
Propachlor	Ramrod	350 ppb[b]	70 ppb[b]
Simazine	Princep	50 ppb	35 ppb
X2,4-D	2,4-D	1.1 ppm	70 ppb
Niscosulfuron	Accent	44 ppm	44 ppm[c]
Primisulfuron	Beacon	210 ppb	210 ppb

[a]Proposed MCL.
[b]Based upon the Reference Dose value for ingestion.
[c]Based upon the Office of Pesticide Policy Reference Dose Value.

human and aquatic vegetation exposure values.

Economic Indicators

A key economic indicator is the change in net returns given an atrazine or triazine ban. Baseline net returns are estimated at $7.8 billion(b), $2.8b, and $5.2b for the Corn Belt, Lake States, and Northern Plains. Banning atrazine results in essentially no change for the Corn Belt, and decreases returns by 2.6 percent and 2.5 percent in the Lake States and Northern Plains. Constant net returns in the Corn Belt results from the introduction of the new technology provided by the low-dosage herbicides of Accent and Beacon introduced in 1990. Herbicide strategies which include these two chemicals are estimated by WISH and RAMS to be extremely profitable in various regions of the country, primarily due to reduced expected yield loss. We discuss this aspect in more detail when presenting state-level results.

A triazine ban reduces net returns in all three regions, ranging from 3.8 percent to 0.5 percent. For the Corn Belt and Lake States, this implies net income decreases by $100 million (m) in each region. The net return in the Northern Plains decreased by $200 m. Decreased average net returns per acre ranges from 0 percent to 2.9 percent for the atrazine ban, and 0.5 percent to 4.1 percent for the triazine ban.

For six representative states decreased, net returns decreased range from 0.6 percent to 4.15 percent for the atrazine ban, and from 1.37 percent to 5.12 percent for the triazine ban, with the noted exception of Missouri. Net returns in Missouri actually increased slightly with both bans. Again, the reason is the predicted adoption of Accent and Beacon into our model. Without Accent and Beacon, an atrazine or triazine ban would undoubtedly reduce net returns. With this new technology available, but still not widely used, we find that relaxing the chemical flexibility constraints in RAMS actually allows the producer to use production activities that increase the use of these new herbicides.

To illustrate, compare the major PAs for Iowa (PA41) and Missouri (PA60). In PA41, in the baseline model atrazine is used on more than five million acres of corn, competing favorably with strategies including Accent and Beacon. With an atrazine ban, the five million acres are now treated by more expensive activities. Therefore, net return decreases. But in PA60, atrazine use in the baseline model was at its lower bound (± 20 percent of estimate atrazine use by Resources for the Future's 1990 herbicide use data). An atrazine ban relaxes the bound in chemical use, allowing the producer in PA60 to use more activities with Accent and Beacon. The gains more than offset the losses of a new constraint on atrazine. While the diffusion of new technology may take time, the results suggest that Accent and Beacon may be increasingly used in parts of the Corn Belt, thereby mitigating the economic consequences of an atrazine or triazine ban. But this result is still under review because of the potential problems associated with Accent and Beacon.

Figure 2-6 shows the changes in overall crop production acreage for the Corn Belt. In the Corn Belt, acreage changes for the atrazine and triazine bans were similar. The major shift is the 15 percent increase in soybean acreage from the baseline of 26 million acres. Corn grain acreage decreased by nearly 13 percent from a base of 43 million acres. Sorghum grain acreage also decreased by about 16 percent from a base of 0.9 million acres. The patterns were similar for the Lake States. Corn grain acreage decreases by nearly 10 percent from a base of 14.6 million acres, while soybean acreage increased by nearly 18 percent from a base of 5.8 million acres.

Figure 2-7 illustrates how the bans affect tillage practices. Given the potentially conflicting goals of reduced soil erosion and reduced chemical use, it is useful to understand the environmental and agricultural policy trade-offs associated with chemical bans. For the Corn Belt (figure 2-7a), we estimate that there are minor shifts in tillage for all crops due to conservation compliance. But we do observe major shifts in tillage on corn acreage. The pattern is similar for the Lake States (figure 2-7b). For corn with an atrazine ban, conventional tillage increases by about 80 percent, while no tillage decreases by nearly 40 percent. The triazine ban has similar, but slightly less dramatic results. Reduced tillage increases for both bans in the Lake States, but has mixed results for the Corn Belt. The pattern of increased conventional tillage (either fall or spring plow) also holds for sorghum acreage in the Corn Belt and Northern Plains. Note that reduced tillage does increase in the Northern Plains for both bans.

The increased reliance on conventional tillage suggest a potential conflict between the goals of soil conservation and reductions in nonpoint herbicide pollution. Banning atrazine or the triazines, increases the reliance on tillage practices that increase soil erosion. Since the EPA regulates herbicides and the USDA administers programs for soil conservation, potential conflicts between agency objectives arise. Interagency cooperation now becomes more important to avoid unilateral action that may diminish the effectiveness of Agency policy at an even greater cost. Game theorists have proven time and time again that unilateral

Figure 2.6 CHANGES IN CROP PRODUCTION ACREAGE
Corn Belt Region

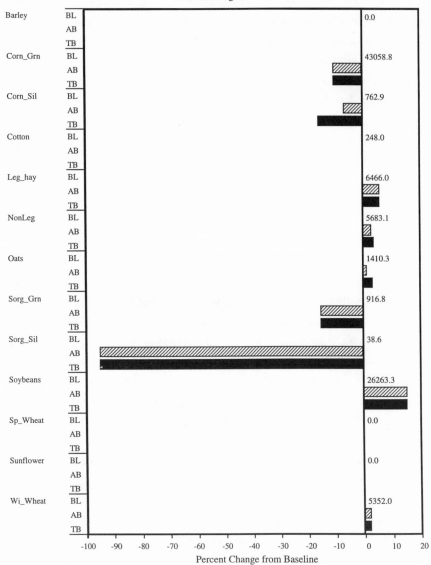

Percent Change from Baseline

Baseline Figures are in 1000_Acres

Figure 2.7 CHANGES IN CROP PRODUCTION ACREAGE BY TILLAGE
Corn Belt Region

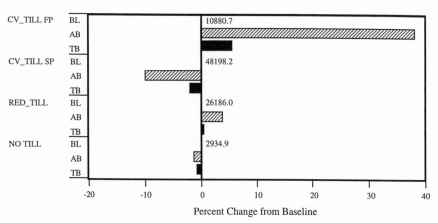

Baseline Figures are in 1000_Acres

Lake States Region

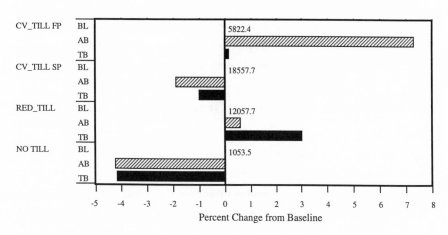

Baseline Figures are in 1000_Acres

actions may well lead to undesired outcomes.   The trade-off between soil
conservation and pesticide source reduction suggests serious consideration must be
given to developing an institution as to maintain and most importantly, reward
interagency decision making.

Figure 2-8 shows the changes in herbicide use on corn for the Corn Belt. For
the atrazine ban, the major gainers are Princep and Prowl, which increase by over
100 percent. Other consistent gainers include Accent, Beacon, and Bladex. For a
triazine ban, the big gainers are 2,4-D, Accent, Beacon, Roundup, and
Suttan/Eradicane.

Environmental Indicators

We now consider how the atrazine and triazine bans affect the chemical
concentrations and exposure values (i.e., the measure of relative risk) for surface
and groundwater. We focus on the relative exposure values to indicate potential
problems. Recall the exposure values normalize the concentrations so that any
value exceeding unity implies the concentration exceeds the EPA benchmark dose
values. If the exposure value is less than unity, the concentration is below the
benchmark. A value considerably below unity--less than 1/100-- suggests that
concentrations of the herbicide might not pose a significant risk.

Chronic Exposure Levels for Groundwater at 15m—Average Analysis

The baseline estimates of corn and sorghum chemical concentration in
groundwater at 15m aggregated to the state level do not exceed the EPA's
benchmark values for any chemical in any region either for peak or average
concentrations. The exposure values do not increase significantly for either the
atrazine ban or the triazine ban. This suggests that nonpoint herbicide pollution in
groundwater is not a major risk. Figure 2-9 illustrates the percentage change for
the Corn Belt by herbicide under conventional tillage practices. Note no chemical
concentration exceeds the EPA's benchmark.

Acute Exposure Values for Surface Water—Average Analysis

The estimates from acute surface water concentration levels do exceed the
benchmark values for several chemicals. But given the assumptions in the model,
the concentrations are likely to overestimate the concentration levels.
Consequently, we put more emphasis on the relative changes in concentrations, not

Figure 2.8 CHANGES IN HERBICIDE APPLICATION ON CORN
Corn Belt Region

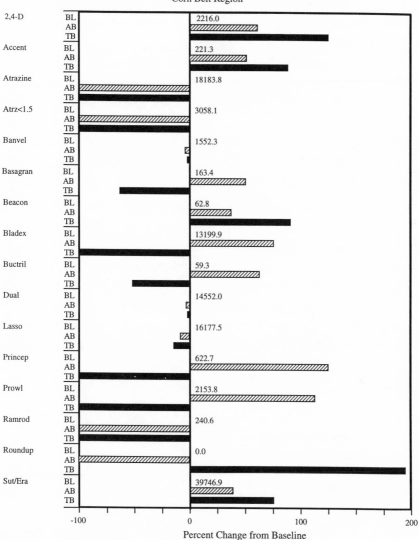

Percent Change from Baseline

Baseline Figures are in 1000_lbs. AI

Figure 2.9 CHANGE IN CHRONIC CONCENTRATION IN THE GW AT 15 MTS
Corn Belt Region, Conventional Tillage

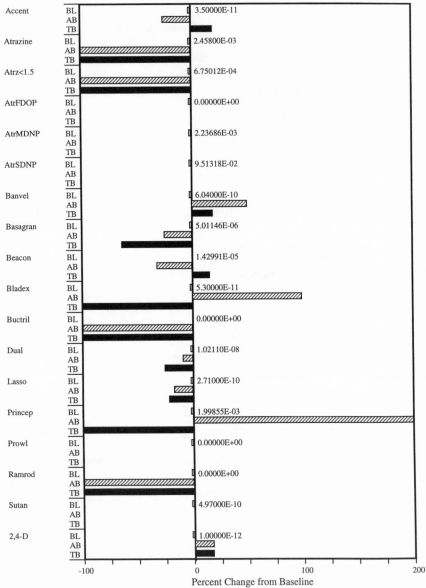

Baseline Figures are in 1000_Acres

absolute levels. Figure 2-10 illustrates the changes in acute concentrations and exposure levels (by tillage) in surface water for the Corn Belt. For corn herbicides, the baseline case estimates the exposure level for atrazine with conventional tillage equaled 1.436 in the Corn Belt. Princep on corn also exceeded the reference dose with an exposure value of 1.467 for conventional tillage. The exposure values for Bladex, Bassagran, and Lasso on corn were the next highest at 0.612, 0.540, and 0.578. For corn herbicides in the Lake States, Princep had the highest exposure value at 1.565 with no tillage. The atrazine exposure values for all tillage practices were below the reference value at 0.414, 0.033, and 0.161 for conventional, reduced, and no tillage. For sorghum herbicides in the baseline model, only atrazine with conventional tillage in the Corn Belt exceeded the benchmark value at 1.05. Lasso with conventional tillage was the next highest exposure level at 0.714 in the Corn Belt. Exposure levels in the Lake States were relatively low.

For the atrazine ban in corn production, we estimate a significant increase in the exposure level for Princep with conventional tillage in the Corn Belt at 3.625, or a 132 percent increase. The Princep exposure level in the Lake States increase to 2.441 from 0.317 from the baseline case, a 670 percent increase. Bladex concentrations under reduced tillage exceed the benchmark value in both the Corn Belt and Lake States. The exposure levels increased in the Corn Belt to 1.712 from 0.744 (130 percent increase) and in the Lake States to 1.707 from 0. With an atrazine ban, the other two triazines, Bladex and Princep, become more attractive for corn production and more of a potential problem in surface water. This pattern is consistent in the Northern Plains where exposure values for Bladex and Princep increase to 1.498 and 1.821 from 0.698 and 0.578 in the baseline case after an atrazine ban. The atrazine ban actually resulted in the increased concentrations of the other two triazines beyond the benchmark.

With an atrazine ban for sorghum, we find that no chemical concentration exceeds the benchmark in either the Corn Belt or Northern Plains. The highest exposure value was 0.746 for Lasso with conventional tillage in the Corn Belt, while exposure values for Dual and Banvel equaled 0.482 and 0.389. In the Northern Plains, the highest exposure levels were registered for Lasso under conventional tillage, 0.545, and Bladex under reduced tillage, 0.513.

In the triazine ban on corn, Princep and Bladex are no longer available to the producer. We estimate that all chemicals under all tillage practices for both the Corn Belt and Lake States have exposure values less than unity. The highest value is for Bassagran under conventional tillage in the Lake States was 0.725, while in

Figure 2.10 CHANGE IN ACUTE CONCENTRATION IN SURFACE WATER
Corn Belt Region, Conventional Tillage

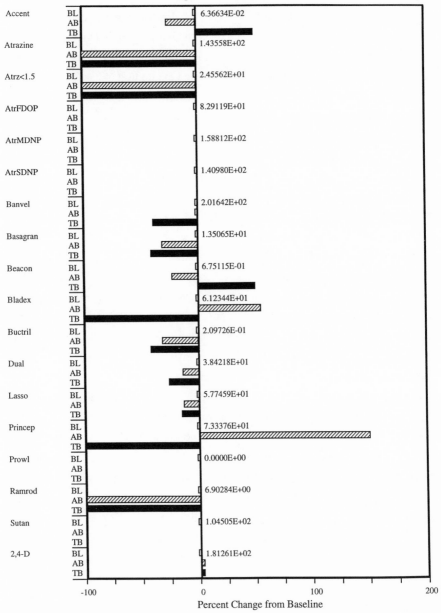

Baseline Figures are in 1000_Acres

the Corn Belt it was 0.368. The two low-dosage herbicides, Accent and Beacon, both have low exposure values in both regions, ranging from 0 to 0.005.

With a triazine ban for sorghum, no chemical concentration exceeds the benchmarks. In both the Corn Belt and Northern Plains, Lasso, Dual, and Banvel under conventional tillage had the highest exposure levels at 0.727, 0.470, and 0.389, and 0.305, 0.409, and 0.535.

Exposure variability

In the previous discussion, environmental exposures were presented for all chemicals and production technologies, aggregated over all soil types in each producing area, giving average indicators at the state and region levels. Under tighter benchmarks than EPA's, for example those at the state level, the average results may still indicate no risk to the environment even though some areas may be more vulnerable than others. In this section we summarize exposure variability as measured by the proportion of soils for which a particular chemical under a particular production technology exceeds the environmental benchmarks. While this measure can then be interpreted as a "probability that any soil is at risk" from a given chemical-tillage combination, it is more intuitively interpreted as a measure of the "spatial distribution of risk," and its usefulness is for targeting particular soils and areas with higher vulnerability.

Table 2-2 summarizes exposure variability for relevant chemicals under the status quo, an atrazine ban, and a triazine ban.[1] The first important thing to note from this table is that only in Wisconsin do we see a small proportion of soils supporting conventional tillage with atrazine concentrations exceeding the groundwater benchmark for chronic human exposure. In addition, we note the atrazine concentrations in surface water which exceed USEPA's benchmark for chronic human exposure for a large proportion of soils (100% in the case of princep) under conventional and reduced tillage, in Iowa, Illinois, Missouri, and Wisconsin. Under no till, only Wisconsin shows a potential problem. Exposure variability under an atrazine ban suggests no concentration exceeds the benchmark value in groundwater. Of particular importance, however, is bladex and princep in surface water in all states under both conventional and reduced tillage. Lasso and Banvel appear to exceed standards only in Illinois. Under a triazine ban, only

---

[1]Note that in Table 2-1 the chemical "atrazine-S" is an atrazine with a slower decay rate, thus susceptible to higher concentrations. This shows sensitivity of the results to the chemical parameters, and in particular, decay rate.

Table 2-2
Exposure Distribution - Percent Exceedence

State	Policy	Chemical	Tillage					
			CT		RT		NT	
			GW	SW	GW	SW	GW	SW
Iowa	Baseline	Atrazine	0.00	53.30			0.00	0.00
Illinois	Baseline	Atrazine	0.00	88.07	0.00	10.20	0.00	0.00
Missouri	Baseline	Atrazine	0.00	80.31			0.00	43.51
Wisconsin	Baseline	Atrazine	0.00	1.15	0.00	0.00	0.00	0.00
Iowa	Baseline	Atraz<1.5	0.00	0.00	0.00	0.00	0.00	0.00
Illinois	Baseline	Atraz<1.5	0.00	2.92	0.00	0.00	0.00	0.00
Missouri	Baseline	Atraz<1.5	0.00	17.44	0.00	0.00	0.00	0.00
Wisconsin	Baseline	Atraz<1.5	0.00	0.00	0.96	9.20	0.00	0.00
Iowa	Baseline	AtrSDNP	0.00	93.53			0.00	0.00
Illinois	Baseline	AtrSDNP	0.24	88.08	0.00	10.20	0.00	0.00
Missouri	Baseline	AtrSDNP	0.00	83.82			0.00	43.51
Wisconsin	Baseline	AtrSDNP	1.47	4.40	0.00	0.00	1.68	0.00
Iowa	Baseline	Banvel	0.00	0.00	0.00	0.00	0.00	0.00
Illinois	Baseline	Banvel	0.00	30.91				
Missouri	Baseline	Banvel	0.00	0.00	0.00	0.00		
Wisconsin	Baseline	Banvel	0.00	0.00	0.00	0.00		
Iowa	Baseline	Bladex	0.00	1.48	0.00	83.76	0.00	0.00
Illinois	Baseline	Bladex	0.00	0.00	0.00	90.51	0.00	0.00
Missouri	Baseline	Bladex	0.00	33.12	0.00	65.21	0.00	0.00
Wisconsin	Baseline	Bladex	0.00	0.00	0.00	21.51	0.00	0.00
Iowa	Baseline	Princep	0.00	100.00				
Illinois	Baseline	Princep	0.00	100.00	0.00	100.00		
Missouri	Baseline	Princep	0.00	100.00				
Wisconsin	Baseline	Princep	0.00	85.34			0.00	74.40
Iowa	Baseline	Lasso	0.00	0.00	0.00	0.00	0.00	0.00
Illinois	Baseline	Lasso	0.00	17.53	0.00	0.00		

Missouri	Baseline	Lasso	0.00	0.00			0.00	0.00
Wisconsin	Baseline	Lasso	0.00	0.00	0.00	0.00	0.00	0.00
Iowa	AtrazBAN	Banvel	0.00	0.00	0.00	0.00		
Illinois	AtrazBAN	Banvel	0.00	48.43				
Missouri	AtrazBAN	Banvel	0.00	0.00				
Wisconsin	AtrazBAN	Banvel	0.00	0.00				
Iowa	AtrazBAN	Bladex	0.00	17.75	0.00	100.00		
Illinois	AtrazBAN	Bladex	0.00	41.36	0.00	80.78		
Missouri	AtrazBAN	Bladex	0.00	77.03	0.00	69.23		
Wisconsin	AtrazBAN	Bladex	0.00	0.00	0.00	100.00		
Iowa	AtrazBAN	Dual	0.00	0.00	0.00	0.16		
Illinois	AtrazBAN	Dual	0.00	0.00	0.00	0.00		
Missouri	AtrazBAN	Dual	0.00	0.00				
Wisconsin	AtrazBAN	Dual	0.00	0.00	0.00	0.00		
Iowa	AtrazBAN	Princep	0.00	100.00	0.00	100.00	0.00	0.00
Illinois	AtrazBAN	Princep	0.00	100.00				
Missouri	AtrazBAN	Princep	0.00	100.00	0.00	100.00		
Wisconsin	AtrazBAN	Princep	0.00	100.00	0.00	46.31		
Iowa	AtrazBAN	Lasso	0.00	0.00	0.00	0.00		
Illinois	AtrazBAN	Lasso	0.00	3.41	0.00	3.82		
Missouri	AtrazBAN	Lasso	0.00	0.00				
Wisconsin	AtrazBAN	Lasso	0.00	0.00	0.00	0.00		
Iowa	AtrazBAN	2,4-D	0.00	0.00				
Illinois	AtrazBAN	2,4-D	0.00	0.00				
Missouri	AtrazBAN	2,4-D	0.00	0.00				
Wisconsin	AtrazBAN	2,4-D	0.00	0.00				
Iowa	TriazBAN	Banvel	0.00	0.00	0.00	0.00	0.00	0.00
Illinois	TriazBAN	Banvel	0.00	19.23	0.00	0.00	0.00	0.00
Missouri	TriazBAN	Banvel	0.00	0.00	0.00	0.00	0.00	0.00
Wisconsin	TriazBAN	Banvel	0.00	0.00	0.00	0.00	0.00	0.00
Iowa	TriazBAN	Lasso	0.00	0.00			0.00	0.00

Illinois	TriazBAN	Lasso	0.00	0.00	0.00	0.00	0.00	0.00
Missouri	TriazBAN	Lasso	0.00	0.00	0.00	0.00	0.00	0.00
Wisconsin	TriazBAN	Lasso	0.00	0.00	0.00	0.00	0.00	0.00
Iowa	TriazBAN	Dual	0.00	0.00	0.00	0.00	0.00	0.00
Illinois	TriazBAN	Dual	0.00	0.00	0.00	0.00	0.00	0.00
Missouri	TriazBAN	Dual	0.00	0.00	0.00	0.00	0.00	0.00
Wisconsin	TriazBAN	Dual	0.00	0.00	0.00	0.00	0.00	0.00
Iowa	TriazBAN	2,4-D	0.00	0.00				
Illinois	TriazBAN	2,4-D	0.00	0.00				
Missouri	TriazBAN	2,4-D	0.00	0.00				
Wisconsin	TriazBAN	2,4-D	0.00	0.00				
Iowa	TriazBAN	Accent	0.00	0.00	0.00	0.00	0.00	0.00
Illinois	TriazBAN	Accent	0.00	0.00	0.00	0.00	0.00	0.00
Missouri	TriazBAN	Accent	0.00	0.00	0.00	0.00	0.00	0.00
Wisconsin	TriazBAN	Accent	0.00	0.00	0.00	0.00	0.00	0.00
Iowa	TriazBAN	Beacon	0.00	0.00	0.00	0.00	0.00	0.00
Illinois	TriazBAN	Beacon	0.00	0.00	0.00	0.00	0.00	0.00
Missouri	TriazBAN	Beacon	0.00	0.00	0.00	0.00	0.00	0.00
Wisconsin	TriazBAN	Beacon	0.00	0.00	0.00	0.00	0.00	0.00

19 percent of the soils in Illinois appear with concentrations of Banvel above surface water benchmarks.

Exposure Values for Aquatic Vegetation

Although the triazine ban succeeded in reducing the exposure values to humans, the potential impacts on aquatic vegetation are another matter. Table 2-3 lists the EPA's toxicity benchmarks for aquatic vegetation by herbicide. For atrazine, the aquatic-benchmark is 2ppb compared to the human benchmark of 100 ppb. Note that the aquatic-benchmark for the low-dosage chemicals, Accent and Beacon, are extremely low at 0.03 ppb while to the human benchmarks are set at 44,000 ppb.

Table 2-3
Toxicity Benchmark Values for Aquatic Vegetation[2]

Pesticide	Aquatic Vegetation
Atrazine	2ppb[a]
Alachlor	1ppb[b]
Bentazon	1 ppb[c]
Bromoxynil	1 ppb[c]
Butylate	1 ppb[c]
Cyanazine	2 ppb[d]
Dicamba	1 ppb[c]
EPTC	1 ppb[c]
Glyphosate	60 ppb[e]
Metolachlor	1 ppb[c]
Paraquat	500 ppb[f]
Pendimethel	1 ppb[c]
Propachlor	1 ppb[c]
Simazine	500 ppb[g]
2,4-D	1 ppb[c]
Accent	0.03 ppb[h]
Beacon	0.03 ppb[i]

[a]Four day average concentrations that should not be exceeded.
[b]LC_{50} = 10 ppb, safety factor = 10.
[c]No data. Default value of 1 ppb used.
[d]EC_{50} = 20 ppb (4 days), 10-fold safety factor.
[e]EC_{50} = 600 ppb, 10 fold safety factor.
[f]EC_{50} = 5 ppm, 10-fold safety factor.
[g]LC_{50} = 500 ppb, 10-fold safety factor.
[h]No data. Based upon value for Beacon
[i]EC_{50} = 0.27 ppb, 10-fold safety factor.

[2]Based upon data supplied in OPP memo entitled "Chesapeake Bay Pesticide Index Pesticide Data Evaluation" undated. USEPA, Office of Research and Development, Environmental Research laboratory, Ambient Aquatic Life Water Quality Criteria for Atrazine, draft, September 1990; and USEPA, Guidelines for Deriving Numerical National Water Quality Criteria for the Protection of Aquatic Organisms and Their Uses, in press.

Figure 2-11 illustrates that for surface water in the Corn Belt, the aquatic-benchmarks are exceeded by nearly every chemical under conventional tillage. Often the acute concentrations are over one hundred times greater than the aqua-benchmark. In the Corn Belt, surface water concentrations of Banvel and 2,4-D are nearly two hundred times greater than the benchmark for the baseline and both the atrazine and triazine bans. Even though the surface water concentrations of Accent and Beacon are extremely low, both exceed the aquatic-benchmark for the Corn Belt and Lake States under all three scenarios.

Concluding Comments

Three factors are critical for effective modeling of nonpoint source pollution in an integrated system. First, one should define the set of both agricultural and environmental policy tools. Accurately defining the set will allow the policymaker to explore the attractiveness of alternative strategies to control the agri-ecological-economic conditions. Second, understanding how producers will substitute inputs given a policy is vital if one is to estimate accurately the costs and benefits of a new policy recommendation. A detailed model of alternative weed control strategies will provide information on the trade-offs associated with price incentives and quantity constraints. Third, when considering a regional or national policy, one cannot afford to run and rerun each modeling system for each new policy. Instead, metamodels can be statistically constructed, thereby minimizing the costs of building an integrated system.

We have illustrated the importance of these issues in the CEEPES system for two policy scenarios—an atrazine and a triazine ban. Overall, an atrazine ban was unattractive due to a decrease in net returns of agricultural producers with no gain in environmental quality. The triazine ban also reduced net returns, but no chemical exposure level exceed the toxicity-weighted benchmark values.

Note that the research requires further analysis of the atrazine and triazine bans. A detailed examination of key states is currently underway. This will allow us to consider in more detail how rotations and tillage practices are impacted by the bans. Also more analysis is required on the variability of exposure levels to determine the percentage of soils exceeding the EPA threshold. This will provide more insight into the probable environmental impacts of the bans.

There are several desirable extensions for future implementation that we are considering. First, we are relaxing the current constraint on atrazine use in corn-soybean rotations. Second, we are revisiting the potential adoption of Accent and

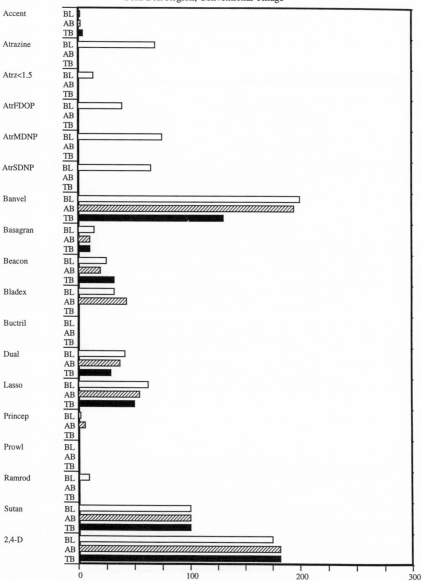

Figure 2.11 ACUTE EXPOSURE LEVELS: SURFACE WATER
Corn Belt Region, Conventional Tillage

Baseline Figures are in 1000_Acres

Beacon. Given both chemicals are relatively new, more analysis is warranted. Third, there are several other policy options such as price incentives and restrictions on use, technology, and timing that will be explored.

References

Anderson, G. *et al.* (1985). "Nonpoint Agricultural Pollution: Pesticide Contamination of Groundwater Supplies," *American Journal of Agricultural Economics* 67:1238-1243.

Barnes, J. (1976). "Hazards to People," in Pesticides and Human Welfare, D. Gunn and J. Stevens, eds. Oxford: Oxford University Press.

Belluck, D.,S. Benjamin, and T. Dawson (1991). "Groundwater Contamination by Atrazine and Its Metabolites: Risk Assessment, Policy, and Legal Implications," in Pesticide Transformation Products, Fate and Significance in the Environment, L. Somasundaram and J. Coats, eds. Washington, D.C.: American Chemical Society.

Bouzaher, A. *et al.* (1990). "A Dynamic Programming Approach to a Class of Nonpoint Source Pollution Control Problems," *Management Science* 36:1-15.

Bouzaher, A., J. Shogren and D. Holtkamp, (1991). Resource Adjustable Modeling System. Mimeo. Center for Agricultural and Rural Development, Iowa State University.

Bouzaher, A., D. Archer, R. Cabe, A. Carriquiry, and J. Shogren (1992). "Effects of Environmental Policy on Trade-offs in Weed Control Management," *Journal of Environmental Management* 36: 69-80.

Bouzaher, A., P. Lakshamaryan, R. Cabe, A. Carriquiry, P. Gassman and J. Shogren (1993). "Metamodels and Nonpoint Pollution Policy in Agriculture," *Water Resources Research* 29: 1579-87.

Braden, J., and S. Lovejoy, (eds.) (1990). Agriculture and Water Quality. International Perspectives. Boulder, CO: Lynne Rienner Publishers.

Cabe, R. *et al.* (1991). "Metamodels, Response Functions, and Research Efficiency in Ecological Economics," CARD Working Paper.

Carsel *et al.* (1984). User's Manual for the Pesticide Root Zone Model (PRZM). EPA-600/3-84-109.

Cohen *et al.* (1986). "Monitoring Groundwater for Pesticides," Evaluation of Pesticides in Groundwater (W. Gainer *et al.* eds.). Washington, D.C.: American Chemical Society.

Dean, J.D., P.D. Huyakorn, A.S. Donigian, Jr., K.A. Voos, R.W. Schanz, Y.J. Meeks, and R.F. Carsel (1989). Risk of Unsaturated/Saturated Transport and Transformation of Chemical Concentrations (RUSTIC). Athens, GA: U.S.EPA.

Donigian, A.S., Jr., and R.F. Carsel (1987). "Modeling the Impact of Conservation Tillage Practices on Pesticide Concentrations in Ground and Surface Waters." Environmental Toxicology and Chemistry 6:241:250.

Donigian, A.S., Jr., D.W. Meier, and P.P. Jowise. (1986). Stream Transport and Agricultural Runoff of Pesticides for Exposure Assessment: A Methodology EPA/600/3-86/011a. Athens, GA: U.S.EPA.

Goolsby, D.A., and E.M. Thurman (1990). "Herbicides in Rivers and Streams of the Upper Midwestern United States." To appear in proceedings of the 46th Annual Meeting of the Upper Mississippi River Conservation Committee,

March 13-15, 1990, Bettendorf, Iowa.

Gardner, B. (1987). "Causes of the U.S. Farm Commodity Program," *Journal of Political Economy* 95:290-310.

Hallenbeck, W., and K. Cunningham-Burns (1985). Pesticides and Human Health. New York: Springer-Verlag.

Holden, P. (1986). Pesticides and Groundwater Quality: Issues and Problems in Four States. Washington, D.C.: National Academy of Sciences.

Iowa Department of Natural Resource (1990). The Iowa State-wide Rural Well Water Survey Design Report: A Systematic Sample of Domestic Drinking Water Quality. Technical Information Series 17:Feb.

Johnson, S., R. Wolcott and S. Aradhyula (1990). "Coordinating Agricultural and Environmental Policies: Opportunities and Tradeoffs," *American Economic Review* 80:203-207.

Jones, C.A., and J.C. O'Toole (1986). "Application of Crop Production Models in Agro-Ecological Characterization," *Agrotechnology Transfer 4*, October.

Larson, B. *et al.* (1991). "The On-Farm Costs of Reducing Groundwater Pollution," *American Journal of Agricultural Economics* 73:1063-1073.

National Governor's Association (1989). Agricultural and Water Quality. Washington, D.C.

Osteen, C., and F. Kuchler (1986). "Potential Bans of Corn and Soybean Pesticides: Economic Implications for Farmers and Consumers." *Agricultural Economic Report 546.*

Reichelderfer, K., and M. Hinkle (1989). Environmental Interests and Agriculture: The Evolution of Pesticide Policy. Political Economy of U.S. Agriculture: Challenges for the 1990s (C. Kramer, ed.) Washington, D.C.

Shogren, J. and T. Crocker (1991). "Cooperative and Non-cooperative Protection Against Transferable and Filterable Externalities," *Environmental and Resource Economics*, 1:195-214.

U.S. Department of Agriculture (1985). Pesticide Assessment of Field Corn and Soybeans: Corn Belt States. Washington, D.C.: Economic Research Service.

U.S. Environmental Protection Agency (1991). Pesticides and Ground-Water Strategy. 21T-1022, October.

Chapter 3
Modeling Environmental and Trade Policy Linkages:
The Case of EU and US Agriculture

David G. Abler
James S. Shortle

Introduction

Concern for the water quality impacts of crop and livestock production has grown dramatically in the US and in European countries in recent years prompting policy makers to consider taking action to address the issue. While industrial and municipal discharges have been brought under increasing control over the past two decades, agricultural sources of water pollutants remain largely unregulated. There are many concerns about the loss of commercial, recreational, and amenity values from sedimentation and eutrophication of fresh and marine waters (OECD, 1991) as well as health risks from nitrates and pesticides in drinking water. Information on the geographic incidence, health, and ecosystem impacts of agricultural pollution is far from complete. However, the existing evidence is more than adequate to support the implementation of pollution control policies for crop and livestock producers.

Although there are exceptions, the principal approach to reducing water pollution from agriculture has been moral suasion, supplemented to varying degrees by technical and financial assistance (OECD, 1989). The limited results from this approach, along with the growing demand for water quality improvements, have led to calls for more effective regulatory and/or incentive mechanisms. Moreover, the growing recognition that farm price and income support programs encourage environmentally harmful production patterns has led to calls for agricultural policy reforms (OECD, 1989). For example, Reichelderfer and Phipps (1988) suggest that farm program changes could improve the environment enough to forestall separate environmental legislation in the US. We believe much the same to be true in the European Union (EU).

Our objectives in this paper are to explore potential environmental gains from agricultural policy reforms in the EU, and economic and environmental linkages between reforms in the US and EU. Our focus on the US and EU is appropriate since they are the two major players in negotiations on the General Agreements on Tariffs and Trade (GATT). While other countries are involved, the US and EU basically determined the course of agricultural policy reform in the

Uruguay Round. We consider recent, extensive proposals to reform the EU's Common Agricultural Policy (CAP). These proposals, which were more sweeping than those ultimately adopted in 1992, would have slashed agricultural price supports and introduced several supply controls. We also consider CAP reforms combined with cuts in US agricultural price supports, as proposed in recent GATT negotiations. In addition, we analyze the impacts of restrictions on fertilizers and agricultural chemicals in the EU.

Our analysis is based on a partial equilibrium simulation model of agriculture in three regions: the US, the EU, and the rest of the world (ROW). There are three commodities in the model: wheat, coarse grains (maize, barley, sorghum, and oats), and soybeans. These commodities account for the vast majority of nitrate pollution from crops in both the US and EU. The base period is 1986-89, a period chosen on the basis of data needs and availabilities. The focus of this paper is on longer run impacts. Thus we rule out any transitory effects of agricultural or environmental policy reform on rental rates on agricultural capital, fertilizer prices, or the prices of agricultural chemicals.

We pay particular attention to factor market effects of trade and environmental policy changes, effects on which very little research has been done (exceptions include Abler and Shortle 1992a, 1992b; Hrubovcak, LeBlanc, and Miranowski, 1990). Yet, agricultural pollution is to a large degree a function of the use of fertilizers and pesticides. The impacts of policy reforms on the use of these inputs will be influenced by responses in fertilizer and pesticide markets, as well as markets for other inputs. Attention to factor markets also permits us to look explicitly at politically sensitive variables such as returns to farm labor and land. We also devote considerable attention to the sensitivity of our results to key supply-side, technical parameters in the model. This is important because of the limited knowledge about most supply-side parameters, especially in the EU.

Our assessment of environmental impacts is based only on the use of fertilizer and other agricultural chemicals in aggregate and per hectare for wheat, coarse grains, and soybeans across the EU and US. These are good indicators of potential gains in regions that now specialize in the production of these commodities. However, policy changes could influence the regional distribution of production and the supply of commodities not included in our analysis. These effects could be especially beneficial in some regions, but it is also conceivable that some areas could be harmed. For example, our present analysis does not include pollution from livestock, which is a major problem in many regions of the US and

EU. In previous work, we have found that CAP reform proposals could exacerbate these problems (Abler and Shortle, 1992b).

The Model

US and EU Supply

There are three goods in the model: wheat, coarse grains, and soybeans. All three commodities are produced in both the US and EU, although EU soybean production is relatively small. There are many other commodities, such as non-soybean grain substitutes in livestock feed, that affect the supply and demand for the three goods in the model. However, econometric estimates of cross-price effects in supply and demand between grains and non-soybean grain substitutes are generally very close to zero (Sullivan, Wainio, and Roningen, 1989).

The production function for each commodity is a two-level constant elasticity of substitution (CES) (Sato, 1967) exhibiting constant returns to scale at each level. At the upper level, the commodity is produced from a composite mechanical input and a composite biological input. Mechanical inputs provide the power needed to tasks such as planting, weeding, and harvesting, while biological inputs provide nutrients and a growth environment. The lower levels generate the composite inputs. The mechanical input is produced from capital, labor, and agricultural chemicals, while the biological input is produced from land, fertilizer, and chemicals. We allocate chemicals to both of the lower level functions because of their dual mechanical (*e.g.*, a substitute to mechanical cultivation for weed control) and biological (*e.g.*, a substitute for natural biological disease resistance) contributions.

The two-level CES production function is parsimonious in parameters and may represent a reasonable approximation at an aggregate level to agricultural production processes (Kaneda, 1982; Hayami and Ruttan, 1985). The two-level CES is more general than the Cobb-Douglas or CES, which restrict all elasticities of substitution to a single value (unity for the Cobb-Douglas). The two-level CES is also more general than farm-level von Liebig response functions, which assume that all substitution elasticities are zero (Berck and Helfand, 1990). Nested CES production functions have proven very popular in the agricultural economics, public finance, trade, and development literature (see Shoven and Whalley, 1984; Decaluwe and Martens, 1988).

Let Y_i be production of commodity i (i = wheat, coarse grains, or soybeans), M_i be the composite mechanical input, and B be the composite biological input. At the upper level,

$$Y_i = [a_i^{\frac{1}{\alpha_i}} + M_i^{1-\frac{1}{\alpha_i}} + (1-a_i)^{\frac{1}{\alpha_i}} B_i^{1-\frac{1}{\alpha_i}}]^{\frac{\alpha_i}{\alpha_i-1}}, \tag{1}$$

where $0 < a_i < 1$ is a distributive parameter and $\alpha \geq 0$ is the Allen elasticity of substitution. Let K_i be capital, N_i be labor, L_i be land, F_i be fertilizer, and X_i be chemicals. At the lower levels,

$$M_i = [m_{iK}^{1-\frac{1}{\sigma_i}} + m_{iN}^{\frac{1}{\sigma_i}} + N_i^{1-\frac{1}{\sigma_i}} + m_{iX}^{\frac{1}{\sigma_i}}(\theta_i X_i)^{1-\frac{1}{\sigma_i}}]^{\frac{\sigma_i}{\sigma_i-1}}, \tag{2}$$

and,

$$B_i = [b_{iL}^{\frac{1}{\beta_i}} L_i^{1-\frac{1}{\beta_i}} + b_{iF}^{\frac{1}{\beta_i}} F_i^{1-\frac{1}{\beta_i}} + b_{iX}^{\frac{1}{\beta_i}}[(1-\theta_i)X_i]^{1-\frac{1}{\beta_i}}]^{\frac{\beta_i}{(\beta_i-1)}} \tag{3}$$

where $0 < m_{ij} < 1$ and $0 < b_{ij} < 1$ are distributive parameters satisfying $m_{iK} + m_{in} + m_{ix} = 1$ and $b_{iL} + b_{iF} + b_{iX} = 1$. The parameter $0 < \theta_i < 1$ captures the contribution of chemicals to the mechanical and biological production functions. The elasticities of substitution are $\sigma_i \geq 0$ and $\beta \geq 0$. There is no jointness between commodities in production. Empirical evidence for US agriculture on jointness is mixed (e.g., Ball, 1988; Shumway, Pope, and Nash, 1984; Chambers and Just, 1989).

Technology is taken as given. In the long run, restrictions on fertilizers or agricultural chemicals would probably induce fertilizer- or chemical-saving innovation (Bohm and Russell, 1985). Cuts in agricultural price supports that increased the price of fertilizers or chemicals relative to other input prices (by reducing land rents and returns to farm labor even more than fertilizer or chemical prices) would have the same effect. However, there is little theoretical work on this issue at the present time and even less empirical work. Impacts of exogenous technical change within the context of the type of model developed here are examined in Abler and Shortle (1991).

The cost function dual to this production structure is also a two-level CES. (An introduction to cost functions and duality is in Chambers, 1988). At the upper level, the cost of production for commodity I (C_i) is a function of the shadow prices of the mechanical and biological inputs, p_{iM} and p_{iB}, and output:

$$C_i = [a p_{iM}^{1-\alpha_i} + (1-a_i)p_{iB}^{1-\alpha_i}]^{1-\frac{1}{\alpha_i}} Y_i. \tag{4}$$

Let r_i be the rental rate on capital, w_i be the wage rate, ρ_i be the rental rate on land, v_i be the price of fertilizer, and μ be the price of chemicals. Then the cost functions for the lower levels are:

$$C_{iM} = [m_{iK}r_i^{1-\sigma_i} + m_{iN}w_i^{1-\sigma_i} + m_{iX}(\frac{\mu_i}{\theta_i})^{(1-\sigma_i)}]^{\frac{1}{\sigma_i}} M_i, \tag{5}$$

and,

$$C_{iB} = [b_{iL}\rho_i^{1-\beta_i} + b_{iF}v_i^{1-\beta_i} + b_{iX}(\frac{\mu_i}{1-\theta_i})^{(1-\beta_i)}]^{\frac{1}{(1-\beta_i)}} B_i, \tag{6}$$

The shadow prices of the mechanical and biological inputs are equal to marginal (and average) production costs: $p_{iM} = \partial C_{iM}/\partial M_i = C_{iM}/M_i$ and $p_{iB} = \partial C_{iB}/\partial B_i = C_{iB}/B_i$. The producer price of a commodity itself equals marginal (and average) cost: $p_i = \partial C_i/\partial Y_i = C_i/Y_i$. Factor demands are obtained from Shephard's lemma.

Capital, fertilizer, and agricultural chemicals are assumed to have perfectly elastic supply curves. In the short run, supply responses are clearly not perfectly elastic. However, over time, resources used in the production of capital, fertilizer, and chemicals can be withdrawn at relatively low cost to nonagricultural uses (Gardner, 1987). Even if longer run supply curves are not perfectly elastic, elasticities are so large that they can be treated as if this were the case.

We assume that the stocks of land used for the commodities are imperfect substitutes for each other, so that rental rates on land differ across commodities. Of course, a given hectare of land can be used for any crop. At the aggregate level, however, our approach recognizes that some land is better suited for one crop than another. The supply of land for the ith crop is a constant-elasticity function of the rental rates for all crops:

$$\ln(L_i) = l_i + \sum_j \varepsilon_{ij} \ln(\rho_j), \tag{7}$$

where $\varepsilon_{ii} \geq 0$ and $\varepsilon_{ij} \leq 0$ for $i \neq j$, and where l_i is a constant.

Like land, we assume that wage rates for labor can differ across crops, and that the supply of labor for each commodity is a constant-elasticity function of wage rates for all crops. In this case, the justification revolves around regional specialization in production and costs to labor mobility between regions. Accordingly, the supply of labor to the ith commodity is

$$\ln(N_i) = n_i + \sum_j \varepsilon_{ij} \ln(w_j), \tag{8}$$

where $\xi_{ii} \geq 0$ and $\xi_{ij} \leq 0$ for $i =/ j$, and where n_i is a constant.

US and EU Demand

We model demand by constant elasticity functions in consumer prices. The demand (Q_i) function for the ith commodity is:

$$\ln(Q_i) = q_i + \sum_j \gamma_{ii} \ln(p_j^c), \tag{9}$$

where p_j^c is the consumer price, q_i is a constant, $\gamma_{ii} \leq 0$, and $\gamma_{ij} \geq 0$ for $j \neq k$. Differences between producer and consumer prices are discussed below.

US and EU Agricultural Policy

The US has three main policies for wheat and coarse grains: a price floor (known as a "loan rate"), an output subsidy (which is the difference between the market price and a so-called "target price"), and a restriction on planted acreage. Farmers must comply with acreage restrictions in order to qualify for price supports. The only major program for soybeans is a loan rate program. During our

For the purpose of evaluating the effects of changes in EU agricultural or environmental policies on the US, it is important to know how US policies would respond. For example, if US target prices remained fixed even in the face of changes in EU policy, impacts on US wheat and coarse grain production would be quite small. To model US policy responses, we assume that the US producer price for the ith commodity (p_i^{US}) is related to the world price (p_i^w) as

$$\ln(p_i^{US}) = \phi_i + \eta_i \ln(p_i^w), \tag{10}$$

where ϕ_i is a constant and $\eta \geq 0$ is a world price transmission elasticity. Since there are no significant policy distortions on the consumer side in the US, the US consumer price is equal to the world price.

US acreage restrictions are difficult to model because of slippage, which is the natural tendency for farmers to idle their least productive land. The result is that the amount of land idled can be considerably less when measured in quality-adjusted acres. We assume for simplicity that acreage restrictions lead to a neutral shift inward in the supply curve for land that may be less than the amount of land actually idled.

In the EU, three policies form the core of price support activities for wheat and coarse grains in the base period. The first is a system of threshold prices that largely insulates EU markets from world market conditions. Variable import levies maintain the difference between threshold prices and world prices. Second, internal prices are supported by government purchases at intervention prices. The intervention prices are somewhat below the threshold prices, and establish a floor for producer prices. Third, export subsidies, known as restitutions, are used to dispose of surpluses on world markets. Given these policies, EU producer and consumer prices of wheat and coarse grains are treated as exogenous.

EU policy during the base period gave soybeans free entry into the EU, so that domestic consumer prices equal world prices. For producers, a "deficiency payment" system is in operation that ensures they receive a fixed price. Thus the EU producer price for soybeans is modeled as exogenous.

Rest of the World (ROW)

For the sake of simplicity, constant-elasticity supply and demand functions are specified for the rest of the world. ROW supply of the ith crop (S_i) is

$$\ln(S_i) = b_i + \sum_j v_{ij}\ln(p_j^w), \tag{11}$$

while ROW demand (D_i) is

$$\ln(D_i) = d_i + \sum_j \omega_{ij}\ln(p_j^w), \tag{12}$$

where b_i and d_i are constants. This specification does not assume that domestic ROW prices equal world prices. Differences between domestic and world prices are incorporated into the price elasticities in a manner described below.

Market-Clearing Identities

The market-clearing identities require that world supply equal world demand for each commodity. Changes in government and private stocks are ignored.

Parameter Values and Data Sources

Base-period quantity and price data for inputs, supplies, and demands are drawn from the USDA sources listed in the references, the Commission of the European Communities (1986-90), Eurostat (1991), and OECD (1990).

US and EU Supply

The distributive parameters in the production (and cost) functions can be obtained in a very straightforward way from the base-period (1986-89) factor shares. Let s_{ij} be the share of factor j in the total cost for good I. For the sake of simplicity, and lacking any clear evidence one way or another, allocate one-half of the share of chemicals to the mechanical function and the other half to the biological function ($\theta_i = \frac{1}{2}$). Then, using the fact that the partial output elasticity of each input is equal to its share of total cost in equilibrium, we obtain

$$a_i = s_{iK} + s_{iN} + \frac{1}{2s_{iX}},$$

$$m_{iK} = \frac{s_{iK}}{a_i},$$

$$m_{iN} = \frac{s_{iN}}{a_i}, \qquad (13)$$

$$b_{iL} = \frac{s_{iL}}{(1-a_i)},$$

$$m_{iF} = \frac{s_{iF}}{(1-a_i)},$$

with $m_{iX} = 1 - m_{iK} - m_{iN}$ and $b_{iX} = 1 - b_{iL} - b_{iF}$. US factor shares are drawn from USDA *Costs of Production* data, while EU shares are based on Stanton (1986), Bonnieux (1989), and Eurostat (1991). Base-period shares are shown in table 3-1.

Elasticities of supply for labor for the US draw on Barkley (1990) and Perloff (1991). We are unaware of published studies for the EU and thus rely on the US estimates here as well. Short-run land supply elasticities are based on econometric evidence summarized in Sullivan, Wainio, and Roningen (1989). For both land and labor, long-run elasticities are double the short-run values.

Substitution elasticities are derived from existing estimates of Allen elasticities of substitution (AES). Let σ_{ij} be the AES between factors i and j. Then, suppressing the subscript for the commodity,

$$\alpha = \sigma_{KL} = \sigma_{KF} = \sigma_{NL} = \sigma_{NF},$$
$$\sigma = a\sigma_{KN} + (1-a)\alpha, \qquad (14)$$
$$\beta = a\alpha + (1-a)\sigma_{LF}.$$

One can also show that σ_{iX}, where i = capital or labor, is a simple average of α and σ_{KN}. Similarly, it can be shown that σ_{iX}, where i = land or fertilizer, is a simple average of α and σ_{LF}.

Several studies have estimated AES for US agriculture, including Binswanger (1974), Brown and Christensen (1981), Chambers and Vasavada (1983), Hayami and Ruttan (1985), Hertel (1989), Kislev and Peterson (1982), and Ray (1982). Published estimates for the EU relevant to our study are much rarer; we draw upon Bonnieux (1989) for France, Becker and Haxsen (1990) for western

Germany, and, for Ireland, Boyle (1981), Glass and McKillop (1990), and Higgins (1986).

Unfortunately, there are four significant roadblocks that must be overcome here. First, point estimates of the AES even from a single study do not satisfy the equalities in equation (14), although the discrepancies in many cases do not appear to be statistically significant. Second, AES estimates differ from one study to another, often substantially. This is especially true of the studies for the EU. Third, separate estimates are not available for individual commodities. Thus we construct averages and apply them to all three commodities in the model.

The fourth problem is that the own-price output supply elasticities implied by these elasticities of substitution are substantially greater than econometric estimates of supply elasticities. Figures distilled from the econometric studies are in Sullivan, Wainio, and Roningen (1989). These supply elasticities depend not only on substitution elasticities but also on elasticities of labor and land supply. However, regardless of the values assigned to the input supply elasticities, the output supply elasticities turn out to be much larger than the econometric estimates.

Rather than throwing out one set of elasticities, we prefer to see them as emerging from different time perspectives. Following Hayami and Ruttan (1985), consider the concept of a metaproduction function, which can be regarded as the

Table 3-1

Factor Shares, 1986-89 (Percent)

	Commodity					
	Wheat		Course Grains		Soybeans	
Factor	US	EU	US	EU	US	EU
Capital	40	35	40	35	40	35
Labor	15	35	10	30	10	35
Land	30	10	25	10	35	15
Fertilizer	10	15	15	15	5	5
Chemicals	5	5	10	10	10	10

NOTE: Rounded to the nearest 5%

envelope of short-run production functions. In the short and medium run, substitution among inputs is limited by the rigidity of existing capital and equipment. In the long run, these constraints disappear and are replaced by constraints on available technical knowledge. The econometric studies, which generally consider year-to-year changes in supply, are probably capturing short- or medium-run effects. On the other hand, the synthetic supply elasticities implied by the substitution elasticities may be tracing out movements along the long-run metaproduction function.

Thus we initially use two sets of substitution elasticities. The first set, representing a short-run perspective, starts with the econometric supply elasticities and works backward to the substitution elasticities. The second set, appropriate for the long run, starts with the substitution elasticities and ends up with supply elasticities. Short-run substitution elasticities for each commodity in both the US and EU are $\alpha = 0$, $\sigma = 0.1$, and $\beta = 0.2$ in the US. Long-run values in each region are $\alpha = 0.5$, $\sigma = 1$, and $\beta = 1.5$. The sensitivity of our results to the substitution elasticities is examined below.

US and EU Demand

Estimates of short-run price elasticities of demand are in Sullivan, Wainio, and Roningen (1989). Long-run elasticities are likely to exceed short-run values as substitutability in livestock feed increases and lags in consumer behavior play themselves out, and thus are set 50% above the short-run values.

US and EU Agricultural Policy

Base-period US and EU agricultural policy interventions are measured using producer (PSE) and consumer (CSE) subsidy equivalents (OECD, 1990). The PSEs and CSEs, which measure the extent to which producers and consumers are subsidized or taxed, are adjusted so that they capture only output price interventions and not "indirect" assistance on the input side. Base-period values are shown in table 3-2. Agricultural policy reforms analyzed below are modeled as adjustments to these PSEs and CSEs.

Price transmission elasticities from world prices to US prices are estimated in Tyers and Anderson (1988). Short- and long-run elasticities for wheat and coarse grains are all reported as unity, indicating that world price changes are transmitted fully to domestic prices fairly quickly ($\eta_i = 1$).

Table 3-2
Output Price Interventions, 1986-89 (Percent)

	Producer Subsidy Equivalent		Consumer Subsidy Equivalent	
Commodity	US	EU	US	EU
Wheat	31	46	0	-40
Coarse Grains	32	50	0	-45
Soybeans	0	59	0	0

NOTE: PSEs and CSEs are adjusted so as to only capture output price interventions. A positive number denotes subsidization, while a negative number denotes taxation.

Rest of the World (ROW)

Equations (11) and (12) express ROW supply and demand as a function of world prices, which in our model are US consumer prices. Price transmission elasticities relating ROW producer and consumer prices to world prices are drawn from Tyers and Anderson (1988). Short-run ROW supply and demand elasticities with respect to domestic prices are taken from Sullivan, Wainio, and Roningen (1989). We combine these domestic elasticities with the price transmission elasticities and average across countries to obtain short-run elasticities of supply and demand with respect to world prices. Long-run supply elasticities are set at twice the short-run values, while long-run demand elasticities are set at 50% above the short-run values.

Policy Scenarios

We focus our attention on four scenarios. The first involves EU agricultural policy reforms called for by the MacSharry plan. We discuss the details of the plan below. The second involves the MacSharry plan plus a comparable reform in US price supports. The last two involve quantitative restrictions on agricultural fertilizers and chemicals in EU given existing agricultural commodity programs.

Commodity Policy Reforms

In July 1991, Agriculture Commissioner Ray MacSharry put forth a sweeping CAP reform proposal to the Council of Ministers (Commission of the European Communities, 1991; Sheehy, 1992). For crops, it called for price reductions, supply controls, compensation measures, and structural measures, phased in over a three-year period. MacSharry's proposal suggested about a 40% cut in support prices for cereals, with corresponding cuts for oilseeds. The cuts actually adopted in May 1992 were much more modest than the original MacSharry proposal (for details see USDA, 1992). However, future budgetary problems and pressure from the US in the GATT negotiations could yet force the EU to adopt something closely approximating the original MacSharry proposal. Thus it continues to be of policy relevance.

In return for cuts in support prices, the MacSharry proposal called for a system of compensatory payments for cereal and oilseed producers. The May 1992 reforms instituted these payments, although at slightly different levels than envisioned in the MacSharry plan. The payments are on a per hectare basis rather than a per ton of output basis, although the extent to which they are decoupled from output is unclear. The per-hectare payment for each cereal farm in a given region is determined by the region's yields rather than the farm's yields, so that at first glance there would appear to be complete decoupling. However, one must still be a "cereal" farmer in order to receive the payments. In other words, a farmer must continue to engage in the production activities (planting, fertilizing, weeding, harvesting, etc.) in which EU cereal farmers typically engage. One cannot qualify for the payments, for example, by simply throwing some wheat seed on a bare patch of land.

"Professional" cereal producers (basically those with at least 20 hectares of land) would only receive compensation if they met the MacSharry plan's supply control requirements. They would be required to set aside a given percentage of their crop area, fixed initially at 15%. Producers would still receive compensatory payments on their set-aside area, up to a 50 hectare limit. However, hardly any producers would exceed this limit, since it requires at least 333 (= 50/15%) hectares of cereals (Eurostat, 1987). "Small" producers (under 20 hectares) would not have to abide by supply controls. Professional producers constitute only about 10% of cereal farms but about 70% of cereal acreage (Eurostat, 1987), so that the actual set aside would be about 10% ($\approx$ 15% × 70%). The May 1992 reforms were fairly close to the original MacSharry plan in terms of supply controls.

Significantly, the key structural measure in the MacSharry proposal is an "agro-environmental" action program. Crop farmers would be compensated for adopting methods that significantly reduce the use of polluting inputs (fertilizers, pesticides, herbicides, etc.). They would also receive aid for desisting from practices harmful to the environment (*e.g.*, irrigation or plowing up meadows). In addition, farmers and nonfarmers in rural areas would be compensated for the environmental upkeep of abandoned agricultural land. The other key structural measure is a generous early retirement program. Over half of EU farmers are at least 55 years old, and nearly a quarter are at least 65 (Eurostat, 1987). The structural measures actually adopted in May 1992 were largely the same as in the MacSharry proposal.

In our analysis we consider only the price reduction, supply control, and compensation measures in the MacSharry proposal, leaving aside the structural measures. The reason is that the structural measures are not spelled out in sufficient detail to model their effects. For example, the agro-environmental action program only specifies upper limits on the aid for reductions in agricultural chemicals per acre. The program does not indicate what actual aid amounts would be, or the conservation measures required to qualify for aid.

For the price reduction and compensation measures, there is uncertainty regarding the extent to which the MacSharry plan would decouple aid to producers from output, as noted above. We consider an intermediate possibility of 50% decoupling in the simulations below: One-half of the 40% price floor cuts are offset by land subsidies, with the other half offset by output subsidies (which, unlike current price floors, raise producer prices while leaving consumer prices unaffected). In line with the MacSharry plan, subsidy rates are chosen so that producer revenues at base-period prices and quantities are unaffected. For the supply control measures, 10% restrictions are imposed on wheat and coarse grain acreage.

In the simulations with US policy reforms, we cut target prices for wheat and coarse grains by 20%. This cut is comparable with the cuts in the MacSharry plan, and is consistent with recent GATT proposals for multilateral agricultural policy reform. However, since US target prices respond fully to world prices in our model, US producer prices might not fall by the full 20%. For example, if world prices rose 5%, then the US cut would only be 15% (= 20% - 5%).

Environmental Policy Reforms

Economists generally think in terms of emissions-based incentives or regulations as solutions to environmental externalities rather than input-based instruments (Baumol and Oates, 1988). However, the nonpoint character of agricultural pollution makes monitoring emissions impractical. Corrective measures must therefore be applied to polluting inputs and/or land use practices (Shortle and Dunn, 1986). Because of the level of aggregation in this study, we limit our analysis in this paper to reductions in fertilizer and pesticide use.

Specifically, we consider 20% reductions in the aggregate use of each input. The 20% figure is large enough to show some impacts and yet not outside the plausible range. Given the technology assumptions of this analysis, the reductions could be accomplished by EU-wide markets for permits to apply the inputs, input taxes, or firm-level input quotas. As long as the alternatives are designed to have the same impact on total input use, the only differences between them would be distributional. Quotas would yield private rents while taxes would transfer these rents to the public sector. The distribution of rents with marketable input permits would depend on how the rights to the permits were initially assigned as well as other details of the permit system. We do not explore these distributional issues here but we do assess the effects that taxes and permits would have on the demand prices of the inputs.

The tendency in US environmental policy is to use regulations (such as quotas) rather than economic incentives (such as taxes), in part because regulations have a lesser impact on producer rents than taxes. This makes them more politically viable. Other reasons have also been noted in the literature (Bohm and Russell, 1985). We recognize that the administrative structure to regulate fertilizer or chemical use via permits or firm-level quotas currently does not exist. A self-reporting mechanism would probably have to be used, raising issues of noncompliance and enforcement that are not dealt with here.

Taxes on fertilizer and agricultural chemicals have been recently introduced in several European countries and have been proposed in several others (OECD, 1989; TEAGASC, 1989). However, there is considerable interest in quotas in Europe, especially on fertilizer. Fertilizer demands are generally inelastic in own prices, at least in the short run (Burrell, 1989). Over this time horizon, large tax increases would be needed to reduce use. At the same time, because fertilizer demands are generally elastic with respect to output prices, commodity price variations could cause wide swings in fertilizer use (OECD, 1989). Quotas are politically attractive because they would be less harmful to farmers while offering greater reliability in environmental protection.

Results

The MacSharry Plan

The impacts of the MacSharry Plan are shown in table 3-3a (product market impacts) and table 3-3b (factor market impacts). The 20% decrease in EU producer prices brings about sharp reductions in EU production. The long run impacts are substantially greater than those in the short run because of greater long-run supply elasticities. EU consumption of wheat and coarse grains rise significantly with the 40% decrease in EU consumer prices for these commodities. The impact in the long run is again significantly larger than in the short run because of the greater long-run demand elasticities. World prices (= US demand prices) for wheat and coarse grains rise modestly as net EU exports fall. The increase in the world price of soybeans caused by the reduction in EU production is small due to the negligible EU soybean market share. EU soybean consumption falls slightly.

Production of wheat and coarse grains in the US and ROW rise along with the world prices of the commodities. The increases are modest in the short run but much larger in the long run, especially in the US. US production of soybeans declines slightly despite the increase in world prices as land and other resources are shifted to wheat and coarse grains.

Land allocated to wheat and coarse grains in the EU falls by the amount of the set-aside. The land allocated to soybeans falls only slightly. The payment of compensation to cereal producers on a per hectare basis with 50% decoupling gives a significant incentive to substitute land for other inputs, moderating the effect of the reduction in output. The reduction in land use in wheat and coarse grains would be less than 10% if there were no set-asides. Demand prices for land fall significantly in response to the reduction in output prices, but supply prices rise substantially in response to the land subsidies.

Reductions in EU labor use by commodity are roughly proportional to the decreases in output in the short run, but substantially more than proportional in the long run. Returns to labor in the EU fall sharply.

The reductions in fertilizer and other chemical use on wheat and coarse grains are slightly more than proportional to the reductions in output in the short run, but significantly more than proportional in the long run. Since the percentage decrease in fertilizer use is much greater than the percentage decrease in land use in each case, the use per hectare falls substantially. The reductions in fertilizer and other chemical use on soybeans are substantially more than proportional to the reductions in soybean production in the short run and long run. Use per hectare

Table 3-3a
MacSharry Plan - Product Market Impacts
(Percentage Change from Base Period)

	Commodity					
	Wheat		Coarse Grains		Soybeans	
Variable	SR	LR	SR	LR	SR	LR
Supply						
US	2	15	3	20	-1	-1
EU	-18	-46	-20	-54	-9	-41
Supply Prices						
US	6	7	6	6	1	1
EU	-20	-20	-20	-20	-20	-20
Demand						
US	-1	-3	-1	-1	0	0
EU	14	21	17	26	-2	-3
Demand Prices						
US	6	7	6	6	1	1
EU	-40	-40	-40	-40	-40	1
Rest of World						
Supply	5	12	4	8	1	2
Demand	-1	-1	-1	-1	0	0

NOTE: SR = short run, LR = long run. Results are rounded to the nearest integer.
US demand price changes are equal to world price changes.

Table 3-3b
MacSharry Plan - Product Market Impacts
(Percentage Change from Base Period)

Variable	Commodity					
	Wheat		Coarse Grains		Soybeans	
	SR	LR	SR	LR	SR	LR
Land						
US	1	2	2	3	-1	-2
EU	-10	-10	-10	-10	-3	-2
Land Rents						
US	20	21	32	21	2	2
EU	-53/241	-43/206	-60/194	-49/263	-59/57	-50/91
Labor						
US	2	10	3	13	-1	-4
EU	-16	-31	-18	-39	-8	-31
Wage Rates						
US	4	10	5	10	2	4
EU	-35	-38	-36	-40	-23	-29
Fertilizer						
US	5	36	6	38	-1	1
EU	-22	-61	-25	-67	-18	-65
Chemicals						
US	3	28	5	31	-1	1
EU	-21	-59	-23	-65	-15	-59

NOTE: See note to table 3-3a for EU land rents (*), the first number is the percentage change in the demand price. The second is the change in the supply price. The different between the two prices reflects the compensatory land subsidies and the land quotes.

falls dramatically given the relative values of the percentage changes in land, fertilizer, and other chemical use.

The results suggest a substantial potential for EU policy reforms to reduce environmental harm from the use of fertilizer and other chemicals in the EU. The producer price decreases combined with the land-based compensation encourage reductions in aggregate use and the intensity of use of these inputs. However, the effects are limited by the set-aside requirements. Beyond environmental benefits, the reforms would benefit EU landowners, consumers, and, assuming the reforms to be successful in capping the growth of the CAP budget, EU taxpayers. However, farm labor is harmed.

While the MacSharry reforms may be good for the environment in the EU, the opposite would be true in the US and perhaps elsewhere. The aggregate level and intensity of use of both fertilizer and other chemicals increase dramatically as US wheat and coarse grain production rise. Production increases are in response to world price increases. The land allocated to these crops increases only slightly, while percentage increases in fertilizer and other chemicals are about the same as output increases in the short run and much greater in the long run. There is little change in resource use in soybeans. On the other hand, US land rents rise modestly for soybeans and sharply for wheat and coarse grains. US wages also increase.

By and large, the existing European literature is skeptical about the effectiveness of either output or input price incentives in reducing agricultural pollution, owing to the assumption of small output supply and input demand elasticities (*e.g.*, Becker, 1991; Burrell, 1989; Dubgaard, 1990; Vermersch, Bonnieux, and Rainelli, 1991). Elasticities are significantly greater in our simulations, leading to much larger effects on fertilizer and chemical usage.

Bilateral Reforms

The impacts of bilateral reforms are presented in table 3-4a (product market impacts) and table 3-4b (factor market impacts). The EU results are equivalent to those discussed above, except for soybean consumption. Despite the MacSharry reforms, EU consumer and producer prices for wheat and coarse grains, along with soybean producer prices, remain insulated from world market conditions. Accordingly, our focus here is on the US impacts.

With the reduction in US support levels, wheat and coarse grain production fall modestly in the short run but substantially in the long run. Soybean production rises slightly as land and other resources are shifted out of wheat and

Table 3-4a
Bilateral Reforms - Product Market Impacts
(Percentage Change from Base Period)

	Commodity					
	Wheat		Coarse Grains		Soybeans	
Variable	SR	LR	SR	LR	SR	LR
Supply						
US	-5	-19	-7	-22	2	3
EU	-18	-46	-20	-54	-9	-41
Supply Prices						
US	-12	-8	-10	-4	-1	0
EU	-20	-20	-20	-20	-20	-20
Demand						
US	-1	-2	-2	-4	1	2
EU	14	21	17	26	-8	-2
Demand Prices						
US	8	12	10	16	-1	0
EU	-40	-40	-40	-40	-1	0
Rest of World						
US	6	17	8	27	-1	-1
EU	-1	-2	-1	-2	0	0

NOTE: See note to table 3-3a.

Table 3-4b
Bilateral Reforms- Product Market Impacts
(Percentage Change from Base Period)

	Commodity					
	Wheat		Coarse Grains		Soybeans	
Variable	SR	LR	SR	LR	SR	LR
Land						
US	-2	-4	-4	-4	2	3
EU	-10	-10	-10	-10	-3	-2
Land Rents						
US	-35	-25	-37	-23	-3	0
EU	-53/241	-43/206	-60/194	-49/263	-59/57	-50/91
Labor						
US	-4	-14	-7	-15	3	7
EU	-16	-31	-18	-39	-8	-31
Wage Rates						
US	-9	-13	-9	-12	-3	-4
EU	-35	-38	-36	-40	-23	-29
Fertilizer						
US	-11	-38	-12	-35	2	3
EU	-22	-61	-25	-67	-18	-65
Chemicals						
US	-8	-32	-10	-30	2	3
EU	-21	-59	-23	-65	-15	-59

NOTE: See note to tables 3-3a and 3-3b.

coarse grains. World prices for wheat and coarse grains rise significantly but there is little change in the soybean price.

Whereas expansion of wheat and coarse grain production increased the aggregate level and intensity of fertilizer and chemical use in the US in the previous case, contraction has the opposite effect. Land allocated to these commodities falls modestly, while decreases in fertilizer and other chemical use are much more pronounced. The increases in resource use in soybean proportion to the increases in production. Again, it is apparent that there can be significant environmental gains from commodity policy reform. However, unless accompanied by decoupled compensatory payments, the approach we have considered here for the US would be much less palatable to US farmers than the MacSharry plan to EU farmers. Wheat and coarse grain land rents fall substantially, with the short run impacts more pronounced than the long run impacts. Soybean land rents are little affected. Wages also fall as the demand for labor is reduced.

EU Fertilizer Reductions

The impacts of a 20% reduction in EU fertilizer use with existing EU farm programs are presented in table 3-5a (product market impacts) and table 3-5b (factor market impacts). EU wheat and coarse grain production fall, with the decline more pronounced in the short run than in the long run. Fertilizer reductions increase unit production costs whether accomplished by quotas, taxes or other incentives. In the case of quotas, unit costs would rise because least-cost input combinations could no longer be used. Taxes or other incentive mechanisms would increase the opportunity cost of fertilizer use. Given fixed producer prices in EU, increased production costs cannot be passed forward to consumers. Instead, factor use and factor prices must fall to restore equilibrium. The short run effects are more pronounced because of smaller short-run elasticities of substitution and factor supply elasticities. The soybean production responses are much smaller than the wheat and coarse grain responses because of soybean's relatively small factor share for fertilizer.

World soybean prices are little affected by the fertilizer reductions because of the small magnitude of the EU supply response and the negligible market share of EU producers. World wheat and coarse grain prices rise modestly with the reduction in EU supplies and give rise to slight increases in US supply.

Because EU producers are unable to shift the burden of the production

Table 3-5a
EU Fertilizer Restrictions - Product Market Impacts
(Percentage Change from Base Period)

	Commodity					
	Wheat		Coarse Grains		Soybeans	
Variable	SR	LR	SR	LR	SR	LR
Supply						
US	1	2	1	2	0	0
EU	-12	-9	-12	-9	-3	2
Supply Prices						
US	-3	-1	2	1	0	0
EU	0	0	0	0	0	0
Demand						
US	-1	0	0	0	0	0
EU	0	0	0	0	0	0
Demand Prices						
US	3	1	2	1	0	0
EU	0	0	0	0	0	0
Rest of World						
US	2	1	1	1	0	0
EU	0	0	0	0	0	0

NOTE: See note to table 3-3a.

Table 3-5b
EU Fertilizer Restrictions - Factor Market Impacts
(Percentage Change from Base Period)

| | Commodity | | | | | |
| | Wheat | | Coarse Grains | | Soybeans | |
Variable	SR	LR	SR	LR	SR	LR
Land						
US	0	0	1	0	0	0
EU	-1	0	-2	0	0	1
Land Rents						
US	8	2	8	2	1	0
EU	-24	-1	-26	-2	-5	1
Labor						
US	1	1	1	1	0	0
EU	-11	-5	-11	-5	-2	0
Wage Rates						
US	-2	1	2	1	1	0
EU	-23	-5	-23	-5	-13	-3
Fertilizer						
US	-2	4	2	3	0	0
EU	-20	-20	-20	-20	-20	-20
EU Fertilizer Demand Price	121	14	107	13	218	18
Chemicals						
US	1	3	2	3	0	0
EU	-10	-6	-10	-7	2	0

NOTE: See note to table 3-3a.

cost increases forward to consumers, EU land rents and wages fall. For the same reasons that the production impacts are less in the long run than in the short run, the short-run impacts on rents and wages are relatively sharp but the long- run effects are relatively mild. With the expansion of US wheat and coarse grain production, US rents and wages rise modestly in the short run but only slightly in the long run.

EU land use is little affected by the reductions. The use of other chemicals on wheat and coarse grains declines modestly, with the short run impact being more pronounced. There is a slight increase in EU chemical use on soybeans in the short run but no change in the long run. The fertilizer restriction therefore has the additional benefit of reducing other chemical use in most cases. Moreover, the relative changes in land, fertilizer and other chemical use are such that the intensity of fertilizer and other chemical use is diminished. On the other hand, US fertilizer and chemical use rises modestly and there is also an increase in the intensity of use on wheat and coarse grains.

Quotas or taxes on fertilizer cause the supply and demand prices of fertilizer to diverge. The supply price is constant by assumption. The demand price increases as producers are forced to use less fertilizer than they would like. The increase in the EU demand prices for fertilizer gives an indication of the magnitude of the tax on fertilizer that would be required to achieve a 20% reduction in aggregate use. The long-run numbers are probably the more policy relevant. While much smaller than the short-run numbers, the long-run figures imply that the required taxes would still be sizeable. Clearly, farmers would find the MacSharry type of reform a much more palatable way to reduce pollution from agriculture.

Reductions in Other EU Chemicals

Results for the 20% reduction in EU other chemicals are given in table 3-6a (product market impacts) and table 3-6b (factor market impacts). The mechanics of this case are identical to those of the fertilizer reductions. However, because the factor shares of chemicals in wheat and coarse grains are much smaller than the fertilizer shares, the product and factor market impacts, while qualitatively similar, are much smaller. The effects in this case are quite modest in the long run and essentially limited to the EU. On the other hand, chemicals constitute a larger share of total cost for EU soybeans than fertilizer, so that the soybean impacts are somewhat larger than in the fertilizer case.

Table 3-6a
EU Fertililzer Restrictions - Factor Market Impacts
(Percentage Change from Base Period)

	Commodity					
	Wheat		Coarse Grains		Soybeans	
Variable	SR	LR	SR	LR	SR	LR
Supply						
US	0	0	1	1	0	0
EU	-4	-2	-9	-6	-9	-6
Supply Prices						
US	1	0	2	0	0	0
EU	0	0	0	0	0	0
Demand						
US	0	0	0	0	0	0
EU	0	0	0	0	0	0
Demand Prices						
US	1	0	1	0	0	0
EU	0	0	0	0	0	0
Rest of World						
Supply	1	0	1	1	0	0
Demand	0	0	0	0	0	0

NOTE: See note to table 3-3a.

Table 3-6b
EU Chemical Restrictions - Factor Market Impacts
(Percentage Change from Base Period)

	Commodity					
	Wheat		Coarse Grains		Soybeans	
Variable	SR	LR	SR	LR	SR	LR
Land						
US	0	0	0	0	0	0
EU	0	0	-2	-1	-3	-1
Land Rents						
US	3	1	5	1	1	0
EU	-17	-1	-30	-3	-27	-3
Labor						
US	0	0	1	1	0	0
EU	-3	-1	-8	-4	-8	-4
Wage Rates						
US	1	0	1	1	0	0
EU	-11	-2	-5	-3	-10	-2
Fertilizer						
US	1	1	1	2	0	0
EU	-3	-1	-3	-5	-9	-5
Chemicals						
US	0	1	1	2	0	0
EU	240	18	130	13	135	14
EU Chemical Demand Price	240	18	130	13	135	14

NOTE: See note to table 3-3a

Sensitivity Analyses

In this section we examine the sensitivity of our results above to the Allen elasticities of substitution (AES) in production in the US and EU. Estimates of other parameters (especially the land and labor supply elasticities) are based on thinner evidence than the substitution elasticities. However, we have found that the results are quite robust to these other parameters. This is not the case for the AES.

For the sensitivity analyses, all the AES were allowed to vary linearly between their short-run (SR) and long- run (LR) values. Thus the analyses show how the impacts of policy reforms change as the AES change. All the other parameters were fixed at the midpoints of their short- and long-run values.

For both the US and EU, the impacts of fertilizer and chemical restrictions are fairly robust to the AES. As the AES change, effects on fertilizer use, chemical use, land rents, wages, and other variables do not change too much. However, the story is much different for the MacSharry plan and bilateral commodity policy reforms, especially in the EU. (As noted above, the supply-side effects of these two reforms are the same in the EU.) In absolute terms, the effects of commodity policy reforms on fertilizer and chemical usage grow as the AES grow. This is to be expected, since output supply curves become more elastic as the AES increase. As supplies become more elastic, impacts of output price changes on the derived demands for fertilizer and chemicals become larger.

Under the MacSharry plan, there is a substantial rise in EU land rents as the AES increase. As noted above, the payment of compensation to EU producers on a per hectare basis gives a significant incentive to substitute land for other inputs. As the AES rise, this substitution becomes easier. On the other hand, there is a significant decrease in EU wages as the AES increase. The explanation is the same as that for fertilizer and chemical usage. As AES, and thus output supply elasticities, increase, inward shifts in the demand curves for farm labor grow more pronounced.

These findings suggest that extreme caution should be used in quantifying the effects of agricultural or environmental policy reforms. The qualitative conclusions discussed above are fairly robust to different values for the AES, but the magnitudes of the effects definitely are not. The findings are disappointing, especially given the dearth of AES estimates for the EU. In the US, although estimates are more plentiful, there are many large disagreements between studies. The bottom line is that EU policymakers are basically operating in the dark, while US policymakers are not too far ahead.

Conclusions

Our principal conclusion is that agricultural policy reform can do much to reduce agricultural pollution in both the US and the EU by shrinking the sector and the use of polluting inputs. This is illustrated by the MacSharry proposal to reform the EU's Common Agricultural Policy. However, unless accompanied by corresponding reductions in US agricultural price supports, the MacSharry plan could induce a significant shift in cereal production and thus fertilizer/ chemical usage from the EU to the US. Given bilateral agricultural policy reforms, levels of fertilizers and chemicals would be significantly reduced in both regions, both in total and per hectare.

As noted above, our conclusions run counter to some of the literature on economic incentives as a means of agricultural pollution control. However, we feel our results make sense given the longer run focus of our model. Given time, significant expansions and contractions in industries can and do take place. The dramatic growth of EU agriculture over the last 30 years under CAP's auspices is testimonial to this fact. Moreover, there are probably significant asymmetries in EU input supplies. For example, while there is little scope for expanding EU crop acreage, land abandonment is likely if CAP changes radically. The MacSharry document recognizes this possibility. In addition, as mentioned above, over half of the EU's farmers are at least 55 years old. Thus, while there may be little scope for expanding the farm labor force, agricultural policy reforms may induce large-scale early retirements.

References

Abler, D. G., and Shortle, J. S. (1992a). "Environmental and Farm Commodity Policy Linkages in the US and EU," *European Review of Agricultural Economics* 19:197-217.

Abler, D.G., and Shortle, J.S. (1992b). "Potential for Environmental and Agricultural Policy Linkages and Reforms in the European Community," *American Journal of Agricultural Economics* 74:775-781.

Abler, D.G., and Shortle, J.S. (1991). "Innovation and Environmental Quality: The Case of EU and US Agriculture," in *Environmental Policy and the Economy.* F. Dietz, R. van der Ploeg, and J. van der Straaten (eds.), Amsterdam: North-Holland.

Ball, V. E. (1988). "Modeling Supply Response in a Multiproduct Framework," *American Journal of Agricultural Economics* 70:813-825.

Barkley, A. P. (1990). "The Determinants of the Migration of Labor out of Agriculture in the United States, 1940-85," *American Journal of Agricultural Economics* 72:567-573.

Baumol, W. J., and Oates, W. E. (1988). *The Theory of Environmental Policy.* Cambridge: Cambridge University Press.

Becker, H. (1991). "Abatement Control in Agricultural Production Systems by Factor Market Interventions," Paper Presented at Annual Meeting of the European Association of Environmental and Resource Economists, Stockholm.

Becker, H., and Haxsen, G. (1990). "Productivity Development and Environmental Effects in Regional Farming Systems of the Federal Republic of Germany," in , *Land Use for Agriculture, Forestry and Rural Development,* M. C. Whitby and P. J. Dawson (eds.), Newcastle upon Tyne: The University, Newcastle upon Tyne.

Berck, P., and Helfand, G. (1990). "Reconciling the von Liebig and Differentiable Crop Production Functions," *American Journal of Agricultural Economics* 72:985-996.

Binswanger, H. P. (1974). "A Cost Function Approach to the Measurement of Elasticities of Factor Demand and Elasticities of Substitution," *American Journal of Agricultural Economics* 56:377-386.

Bohm, P., and Russell, C. S. (1985). "Comparative Analysis of Alternative Policy Instruments." in: *Handbook of Natural Resource and Energy Economics.* A. V. Kneese and J. L. Sweeny (eds.), New York: Elsevier, 395-460.

Bonnieux, F. (1989). "Estimating Regional-Level Input Demand for French Agriculture Using a Translog Production Function," *European Review of Agricultural Economics* 16:229-241.

Boyle, G. (1981). "Input Substitution and Technical Change in Irish Agriculture - 1953-1977," *Economic and Social Review* 12:149-161.

Brown, R. S., and Christensen, L. S. (1981). "Estimating Elasticities of Substitution in a Model of Partial Static Equilibrium: An Application to U.S. Agriculture, 1947 to 1974," in: *Modeling and Measuring Natural Resource Substitution.* E. R. Berndt and B. C. Field (eds.), Cambridge:

MIT Press.

Burrell, A. (1989). "The Demand for Fertilizer in the United Kingdom," *Journal of Agricultural Economics* 40:1-20.

Chambers, R. G. (1988). *Applied Production Analysis: A Dual Approach.* Cambridge: Cambridge University Press.

Chambers, R. G., and Just, R. E. (1989). "Estimating Multioutput Technologies," *American Journal of Agricultural Economics* 71:980-995.

Chambers, R. G., and Vasavada, U. (1983). "Testing Asset Fixity for U.S. Agriculture," *American Journal of Agricultural Economics* 65:761-769.

Commission of the European Communities. (1991). *Communication of the Commission to the Council and to the European Parliament: The Development and Future of the Common Agricultural Policy*, COM(91) 258. Brussels: Commission of the European Communities.

Commission of the European Communities. (1986-90). *The Agricultural Situation in the Community.* Brussels: Commission of the European Communities.

Decaluwe, B., and Martens, A. (1988). "CGE Modeling and Developing Economies: A Concise Empirical Survey of 73 Applications to 26 Countries," *Journal of Policy Modeling* 10:529-568.

Dubgaard, A. (1990). "Economic Instruments for an Environmental Agricultural Policy in the European Context," *Economic and Fiscal Incentives as a Means of Achieving Environmental Policy Objectives.* Hearing of the Committee on the Environment, Public Health, and Consumer Protection, European Parliament, Brussels.

Eurostat. (1991). *Economic Accounts for Agriculture and Forestry, 1984-1989.* Brussels: Statistical Office of the European Communities.

Eurostat. (1987). *Farm Structure, 1985 Survey: Main Results.* Brussels: Statistical Office of the European Communities.

Gardner, B. L. (1987). *The Economics of Agricultural Policies.* New York: McGraw-Hill.

Glass, J. C., and McKillop, D. G. (1990). "Production Interrelationships and Productivity Measurement in Irish Agriculture," *European Review of Agricultural Economics* 17:271-287.

Hayami, Y., and Ruttan, V. W. (1985). *Agricultural Development: An International Perspective.* Baltimore: Johns Hopkins University Press.

Hertel, T. W. (1989). "Negotiating Reductions in Agricultural Support: Implications of Technology and Factor Mobility," *American Journal of Agricultural Economics* 71:559-573.

Higgins, J. (1986). "Input Demand and Output Supply on Irish Farms - A Micro-Economic Approach," *European Review of Agricultural Economics* 13:477-493.

Hrubovcak, J.; LeBlanc, M.; and Miranowski, J. (1990). "Limitations in Evaluating Environmental and Agricultural Policy Coordination Benefits," *American Economic Review* 80:208-212.

Kaneda, H. (1982). "Specification of Production Functions for Analyzing Technical Change and Factor Inputs in Agricultural Development,"

Journal of Development Economics 11:97-108.

Kislev, Y., and Peterson, W. (1982). "Prices, Technology and Farm Size," *Journal of Political Economy* 90:578-595.

OECD. (1991). *The State of the Environment.* Paris: OECD.

OECD. (1990). *Agricultural Policies, Markets, and Trade: Monitoring and Outlook.* Paris: OECD.

OECD. (1989). *Agricultural and Environmental Policies: Opportunities for Integration.* Paris: OECD.

Perloff, J. M. (1991). "The Impact of Wage Differentials on Choosing to Work in Agriculture," *American Journal of Agricultural Economics* 73:671-680.

Ray, S. C. (1982). "A Translog Cost Function Analysis of U.S. Agriculture, 1939-77," *American Journal of Agricultural Economics* 64:490-498.

Reichelderfer, K., and Phipps, T. T. (1989). *Agricultural Policy and Environmental Quality.* Washington, DC: Resources for the Future, 1988.

Sato, K. (1967). "A Two-Level Constant-Elasticity-of-Substitution Production Function," *Review of Economic Studies* 34:201-218.

Sheehy, S. J. (1992). Personal communication to J. S. Shortle regarding the MacSharry plan. University College Dublin, Ireland.

Shortle, J. S., and Dunn, J. W. (1986). "The Relative Efficiency of Agricultural Nonpoint Pollution Control Policies," *American Journal of Agricultural Economics* 68:668-677.

Shoven, J. B., and Whalley, J. (1984). "Applied General-Equilibrium Models of Taxation and International Trade: An Introduction and Survey," *Journal of Economic Literature* 22:1007-1081.

Shumway, C. R.; Pope, R.; and Nash, E. (1984). "Allocatable Fixed Inputs and Jointness in Agricultural Production: Implications for Modeling," *American Journal of Agricultural Economics* 66:72-78.

Stanton, B. F. (1986). *Production Costs for Cereals in the European Community: Comparisons with the United States, 1977-1984.* Cornell University Agricultural Economics Research Report 86-2.

Sullivan, J.; Wainio, J.; and Roningen, V. (1989). *A Database for Trade Liberalization Studies.* US Department of Agriculture, Economic Research Service Staff Report AGES89-12.

TEAGASC (The Agriculture and Food Development Authority, Ireland). (1989). *Intensive Farming and the Impact on the Environment and the Rural Economy of Restrictions on the Use of Chemical and Animal Fertilizers.* Brussels: Commission of the European Communities.

Tyers, R., and Anderson, K. (1988). "Imperfect Price Transmission and Implied Trade Elasticities in a Multi-Commodity World," in: *Elasticities in International Agricultural Trade.* C. A. Carter and W. H. Gardiner (eds.), Boulder: Westview Press, 255-295.

US Department of Agriculture. (1992). *Western Europe Agriculture and Trade Report.* Economic Research Service, RS-92-4. Washington, DC:

Government Printing Office.

US Department of Agriculture. (1991). *PS&D View Database.* Computer Diskettes.

US Department of Agriculture. (1986-90). *Agricultural Statistics.* Washington, DC: US Government Printing Office.

US Department of Agriculture. (1986-90). *Economic Indicators of the Farm Sector: Costs of Production.* Washington, DC: US Government Printing Office.

Vermersch, D.; Bonnieux, F.; and Rainelli, P. (1991). "Can We Expect Abatement of Agricultural Pollution Using Economic Incentives? The Case of Intensive Livestock Farming in France," Paper Presented at Annual Meeting of the European Association of Environmental and Resource Economists, Stockholm.

Chapter 4
Modeling Ecosystem Constraints
in the Clean Water Act : A Case Study in
Clearwater National Forest

Philip F. Roan
Wade E. Martin

Introduction

An important policy issue is the relationship between ecosystem management and the Clean Water Act (CWA). This paper considers the relationship in the context of a stream ecosystem subject to mineralized discharge from mining waste. Although ecosystem management is not currently incorporated into the language of the CWA, the current focus on sustainable development may move it into the mainstream of the policy debate. In almost all of the provisions of the CWA, the Environmental Protection Agency (EPA) is required to consider the costs of controlling pollution[1]. The second part of this chapter develops a model for calculating the costs of various levels of ecosystem protection by combining site-specific information with existing command and control discharge standards. This model is applied to a hypothetical mine[2] to calculate the costs associated with the barrier to entry ecosystem protection poses for new mines and the reduction in rent at existing mines. These policy impacts represent the principle costs the EPA would need to consider in expanding existing legislation to include ecosystem management.

Background

Section 101 states the goals of the Clean Water Act. In part, these goals are to "restore and maintain the chemical, physical, and biological integrity of the nation's waters". For most of the history of the Act, policymakers have interpreted biological integrity on a species-by-species basis. Since many species exist in a complex relationship with other species, it might be more appropriate to consider biological integrity as the entire system of inter-relationships between various species. Obviously, the system of interrelationships could go far beyond issues

---

[1]Although EPA is required to consider the costs, it is not required to balance them against the benefits in all cases under the CWA.

[2]Cost information for the hypothetical mine is from the U.S. Bureau of Mines.

associated with the Clean Water Act. In order to stay within the framework of the Act, the first abstraction will be to artificially define a sub-system of the global ecosystem that encompasses only water quality issues. True ecosystem constraints would balance the impact of all actions on all species according to some behavioral criterium; most likely maximizing social utility over the set of affected species.

The detailed biological information for determining the impacts, and thus the interspecies trade-offs, is not currently available. Therefore, command and control effluent standards, such as those developed by EPA for section 307 toxic pollutants, are used in the case study. Site-specific information is combined with the effluent constraints to make ecosystem constraints. The Clean Water Act makes the EPA responsible for setting effluent standards on a chemical-by-chemical and industry-by-industry basis. In most cases the EPA has to balance costs against benefits in setting these standards[3]; in other cases[4], the costs do not have to be fully balanced by the benefits, but they must be considered. For new firms, EPA is also directed to consider alternate operating procedures which may better protect the environment.

The model developed in the following section determines optimal operating procedures as well as quantifying the costs of ecosystem protection. Increased ecosystem protection affect firms in two ways: rents will be reduced to existing firms and new firms will face a barrier to entry. For mining firms the barrier to entry can be qualified in terms of the average quality of the ore a new mine must find in order to pay for its factors of production. Geostatistical hypothesis about the size of a nation's mineral deposits can be used to estimate the portion of a nation's mineral wealth that occurs in grades too low to be extracted under the barrier to entry. Thus the barrier to entry can be qualified in terms of the amount of a nation's mineral wealth left in the ground. The case study below will use the example of a small open pit gold mine to illustrate the effects of both the barrier to entry and the reduction in rents. The small open pit gold mine was chosen because it is a common mine type in the western United States.

The Model

An important way in which the mine interacts with the ecosystem of

---

[3]Mostly in the regulation of existing pollution sources as discussed in section 301(b).

[4]Typically new sources covered under section 306 and toxic pollutants under section 307.

nearby streams is by exposing heavily mineralized waste material to rainfall which results in mineralized run-off that enters nearby streams. The positively-charged metallic ions (cations) in the run-off poison various stream animals (similar to arsenic poisoning in humans) but are particularly debilitating to macroinvertebrates. Since macroinvertebrates are near the bottom of the food chain in the stream, their death causes the ecosystem of the stream to lose the ability to support life above the macroinvertebrate level. This simple relationship will be the abstraction of the ecosystem for the model in this chapter. More elaborate environmental models can be constructed to describe the effects of cation migration into surface waters but this relationship captures the essence of the problem. Obviously, considering only this limited ecosystem interaction neglects complex predator-prey relationships in the aquatic food chain as well as interactions between aquatic and non-aquatic animals[5]. This assumption is therefore the first simplification that restricts ecosystem issues to those actions covered under the Clean Water Act.

The problem facing the mine manager is how to optimally manage the mine waste pile and the reserves of ore. The mine extracts a mass of ore, $q(t)$, from a stock of ore, $X(t)$. At the mill, a constant fraction, b ($0 \le b \le 1$), of the ore is separated and sold as a mineral commodity. The b parameter is upper-bounded by the mass fraction of mineral commodity in the ore. Its value is determined by ore grade and mining and milling technology. The assumption that b is constant implies that a constant level of technology is used over the life of the mine. With constant technology, changes in b are caused by changes in ore grade. This assumption will be important later when the question of the minimum required ore grade for a particular mine is explored. The mill adds material to the waste pile in the amount aq where $a \ge 1-b$. The parameter a accounts for mass gained by the ore in the milling process as well as overburden material exposed when the ore is extracted. If $a = 1-b$ then the milling process would add no mass to the processed ore and no overburden material would be exposed when the ore was extracted. This situation is ideal but impossible with current technology.

A constant fraction of the mass of material in the waste pile is assumed to migrate into the stream as metallic cations. The constant, k, relates the size of the waste pile to the amount of metal released into the stream. This model was chosen

---

[5]For example, humans who catch and eat fish exposed to high levels of mercury.

since there is a small body of empirical work that the U.S. Bureau of Mines has done to determine some values for these constants. Constants are available for only a few rock types and generally only for sulfate migration[6]. Since rainfall is the primary mechanism for metal migration, k is a function of the average rainfall for the area in which the mine is located as well as the chemical characteristics of the rock in the waste pile and the chemical processes used in milling the ore. Thus the constant k introduces some site specific information into the model but another piece of information is required before the ecosystem constraint is complete.

The final bit of site-specific information relates to the stream under consideration. Water from upstream of the waste pile and rainfall will serve to dilute the concentration of metallic cations in the stream. Therefore, information on rainfall and stream flow will have to be included in the constraint. With this information, the concentration of metal in the stream can be written as:

$$E(t) = \frac{kW(t)}{R(t) + S(t)} \tag{1}$$

Where the total metal mass added to the stream is kW(t), the fresh water stream flow (assuming there is no polluter upstream of the mine) is S(t), and the volume of fresh water from rainfall is R(t). Equation (1) is the ecosystem constraint. As long as $E(t) \leq E_c$, where E_c is the threshold concentration[7], the constraint is not violated. For the model in this chapter, it will be easier to eliminate E(t) as a variable by writing (1) as a constraint on the size of the waste pile:

$$W_c(t) = \frac{[R(t) + S(t)]E_c}{k} \tag{2}$$

Therefore the ecosystem constraint will be satisfied if the mass of the waste pile remains below the critical level defined in (2).

The waste pile is under the control of the mine manager. It increases with ore extraction and decreases as waste is reclaimed or when metals migrate from the

---

[6]The constants used in the case study are for sulfate migration from iron-ore waste rock. This is a gross simplification of the constants that should have been used, namely cation migration from gold-bearing rock but such constants were not available.

[7]These are EPA's published effluent standards. For an example, see EPA [13] table 2.

waste pile into the stream. Reclaimed material is assumed to be perfectly isolated from the drainage. The dynamic of the mass of the waste pile is described by:

$$\dot{W} = aq(t) - r(t) - kW(t) \qquad (3)$$

The final term in (3) represents the mass of waste that migrates into the stream.

The second state variable is the stock of ore in the ground which decreases when ore is extracted. This formulation ignores new discoveries of ore and changes in the effective size of the orebody due to changing extraction technology. Following the traditional Hotelling [7] model, the transition relationship is

$$\dot{X} = -q \qquad (4)$$

The control variables are q(t), the amount of ore extracted and r(t), the amount of waste reclaimed. Both control variables are required to be non-negative and limited by installed capital which is assumed to be constant.

$$0 \le q \le q_{max} \qquad (5)$$

$$0 \le r \le r_{max} \qquad (6)$$

The mine manager is assumed to select q(t) and r(t) to maximize the sum of discounted profits from the mine over a free time horizon using a constant discount rate, δ. Initial and final levels of ore are known, as is the initial level of waste. The final level of waste is free. The problem for the mine manager in a perfectly competitive market is

$$\max_{\{q,r\}} \int_0^T e^{-\delta t} \{pbq(t) - C[q(t)] - A[r(t)]\} dt \qquad (7)$$

subject to:

$$W(t) \le W_c(t) \qquad (8)$$

$$W(t) \geq 0 \qquad\qquad\qquad (9)$$

$$X(t) \geq 0 \qquad\qquad\qquad (10)$$

and (3) - (6), where:

       T is the operating life of the mine (free),

       p is the price of the mineral commodity (assumed constant),

       $C[q(t)]$ is the cost of extracting ore, and

       $A[r(t)]$ is the abatement cost, the cost of reclaiming waste.

All other variables and endpoint conditions are as described above.

The fact that the extraction cost function depends only on the amount extracted implies that the orebody is homogenous. Such a cost function is well-suited to mining for disseminated ore such as occurs in many gold deposits in western states[8]. The abatement cost function depends only on the amount of waste reclaimed. This implies that the waste is also homogenous which is consistent with the previous assumption of homogenous ore.

The current-valued Hamiltonian (suppressing time arguments) is

$$\tilde{H} = pbq - C(q) - A(r) - \mu_X q + \mu_W[aq - r - kW] + \lambda(W_c - W) \qquad (11)$$

where:

      μ_W is the current-valued shadow price of mine waste.

      μ_X is the current-valued shadow price of ore in the ground.

      λ is the current-valued shadow price of an additional unit of environmental slack and is required to be a non-negative function of time. The general solution to this problem is relatively straight forward using the maximum principle. The solution reported here will be based upon specific functional forms from the U.S. BOM. [9]

---

[8]Disseminated ore is common in open pit mines as opposed to veins of ore typically found in underground mines. Normally, underground mines will be subject to stock effects and open pit mines will not.

[9]See Roan and Martin (1996) for more detail on the solution.

Linear Cost Functions

A question that occurs to people familiar with mining operations and the theory of optimal depletion of exhaustible resources is why mine managers never seem to tilt production toward the earlier portion of the life of the mine as theory would suggest they should. Instead, mine managers generally try to run their operations as close to maximum capacity as possible. Two explanations for this behavior are consistent with economic theory. First, mine managers may have zero discount rates. This would be consistent with uniform extraction rates over the life of the mine but seems unlikely and while it would be consistent with models of the mine as a single product firm, it would be inconsistent with the above model. Second, mine managers may act as if they had linear cost functions. This would correspond to a "bang-bang" solution in optimal control theory.

Mine managers may believe their cost functions are nonlinear, but the uncertainty in measuring the costs in a complex system like a mine may encourage mine managers to adopt the simplifying assumption of linear costs at least over the portion of the operating range of concern. The U.S. Bureau of Mines has constructed linear cost models for nine different mining methods and six milling methods. Since these models will be used for the application in the next section, this section will incorporate linear cost functions into the model.

Consider the following forms for $C(q)$ and $A(r)$:

$$C(q) = C_0 + C_1 q$$

$$A(r) = A_0 + A_1 r$$

Using these cost functions, the Hamiltonian will be linear in the choice variables, and the marginal rules will become switching equations:

$$q = \begin{cases} q_{max} \\ q* \\ 0 \end{cases} \quad if \quad -\mu_W(t) \begin{cases} < \\ = \\ > \end{cases} \begin{cases} \dfrac{pb - C_1 - \mu_X(t)}{a} \end{cases} \tag{12}$$

$$r = \begin{cases} r_{max} \\ r* \\ 0 \end{cases} \quad if \quad -\mu_W(t) \begin{cases} > \\ = \\ < \end{cases} A_1 \tag{13}$$

Where the asterisks indicate singular paths. If either (12) or (13) hold with equality for more than an instant of time, a singular path for q or r exists. From (12) and (13), we see that the assumption that a singular path exists for either variable leads to the contradiction that a constant is equal to an exponential for more than one unique instant. Therefore, singular paths cannot exist and the behavior of q and r is undefined at the instant when (12) and (13) hold with equality but is defined everywhere else.

The switching criterium is more obvious after rearranging (26):

$$q = \left\{ \begin{matrix} q_{max} \\ 0 \end{matrix} \right\} \ if \ pb \left\{ \begin{matrix} > \\ < \end{matrix} \right\} C_1 + \mu_x(t) - a\mu_w(t) \qquad (14)$$

Ore should be extracted at the maximum rate as long as the marginal revenue exceeds the marginal cost of extraction and the user costs associated with the stock of ore and the stock of environmental slack.

The interpretation of (13) is to reclaim at the maximum rate whenever the marginal cost of reclamation is less than the user cost of consuming environmental slack (again, interpreting the negative of a negative shadow price as a positive user cost). In other words, if it is cheaper to make environmental slack than to consume from stock, reclaim at the maximum rate. If the marginal cost of reclamation exceeds the user cost of consuming environmental slack, the optimal level of reclamation is zero.

Assuming the initial value of the current-valued shadow price of mine waste is negative and greater than the switching value for each control variable, we see from (12) and (13) that q will start at q_{max} and later switch to zero; r will start at zero and later switch to r_{max}. Designating the time when r switches from zero to r_{max} as t_r and the time when q switches from q_{max} to zero as t_q, we can identify three distinct cases depending on whether $t_r <$, $=$, or $> t_q$. These three cases are presented below as plots of (12) and (13).

Case one ($t_r < t_q$): This case can be characterized by the behavior of the control variables in each of its three sub periods (figure 4-1). The first sub-period, $0 \leq t \leq t_r$, is characterized by the following values of the control variables: $r = 0$ and $q = q_{max}$. During the first sub-period, the amount of ore in the ground decreases with cumulative extraction

$$X(t) = X_0 - q_{max} t \qquad (15)$$

Figure 4-1 Case One: tr < tq

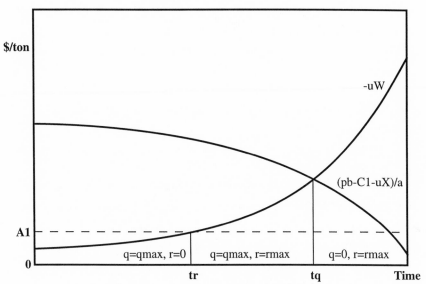

The waste pile behaves according to

$$W(t) = \frac{aq_{max}}{k} + \left(W_0 - \frac{aq_{max}}{k} \right) e^{-kt} \tag{16}$$

To determine whether the waste pile grows or shrinks, we take the time derivative of (16) which yields:

$$\dot{W} = (aq_{max} - kW_0)e^{-kt} \tag{17}$$

Equation (17) shows that the waste pile will increase, decrease, or remain constant in the initial period depending on the initial size of the waste pile. If the initial size of the waste pile is big enough so that the mass lost to metal migration from rainfall is greater than the mass added by extraction at the maximum rate, the waste pile will shrink in the initial period. This seems highly unlikely, and the assumption that the waste pile will grow in the initial period seems more realistic.

Suppose the waste pile reaches the critical size, W_c, in this sub-period at time t_c. Then the constraint becomes active and the solution changes from a bang-bang solution to a constrained solution. When the constraint is active, the control variables can assume values other than the extremes of their control ranges. The question then becomes what values of q and r are optimal during the constrained solution. If it is unprofitable to be on the state-space boundary at q_{max} then, with linear cost functions, it will be unprofitable to be on the boundary at any level of extraction. If it is profitable to stay on the boundary, then the argument in the appendix to this chapter demonstrates why extraction should remain at q_{max} for the constrained solution and reclamation should be adjusted to maintain the waste pile at its critical size from t_c until the terminal time, T.

Continuing with the analysis of case one, if the waste pile does not hit the critical level in the initial subperiod, a second subperiod occurs. The second subperiod, $t_r \le t \le t_q$, has the following values for the control variables: $r = r_{max}$ and $q = q_{max}$ (figure 4-1). The amount of ore in the ground continues to decrease:

$$X(t) = X_0 - q_{max}t \tag{18}$$

The waste pile behaves according to:

$$W(t) = \left(W_0 + \frac{r_{max}e^{kt_r} - aq_{max}}{k} \right) e^{-kt} + \frac{aq_{max} - r_{max}}{k} \qquad (19)$$

Differentiating (19) with respect to time yields:

$$\dot{W} = (aq_{max} - kW_0)e^{-kt} - r_{max}e^{kt_r - t} \qquad (20)$$

The waste pile will increase, decrease, or remain constant depending on whether the right-hand side of equation (20) is positive, negative, or zero. In the first subperiod we argued that the quantity in parenthesis in (20) is positive so the question comes down to the magnitudes of the two components on the right hand side of (20). Below, it will be demonstrated that if the waste pile decreases in this subperiod, the problem is unconstrained. Assuming the waste pile continues to increase, consider the possibility that it hits the critical level during this subperiod. Since the waste pile is increasing even with r at r_{max}, q will have to be reduced to q_c as defined in the appendix in order for the waste pile to stay on the state-space boundary. If the waste pile does not hit the critical level in the second subperiod, then the third and final subperiod in case one occurs.

The third subperiod, $t_q \leq t \leq T$, has the control variables set at q=0, and r=r_{max} (figure 4-1). The waste pile shrinks in this subperiod since its equation of motion is now:

$$\dot{W} = -r_{max} - kW \qquad (21)$$

Therefore, if the waste pile doesn't hit it's critical level in the first two subperiods, it never will. If the waste pile never hits the critical level then the solution corresponds to the unconstrained solution which has been thoroughly analyzed in the traditional mining literature (Burness, 1976). From the necessary conditions it can be seen that at the unconstrained solution $\mu_W(0) = 0$, as was argued in section 2, thus no switching occurs; q = q_{max} and r = 0 for the entire period of case one. Cases two and three are similar to case one.

Case two, $t_r = t_q$, (figure 4-2) has only two subperiods. During the first subperiod the state variables behave just as they do in the first subperiod of case one. During the second subperiod, they behave just as in the final subperiod of case one. Therefore, in case two, if the constraint does not become binding in the

Figure 4-2 Case Two: tr = tq

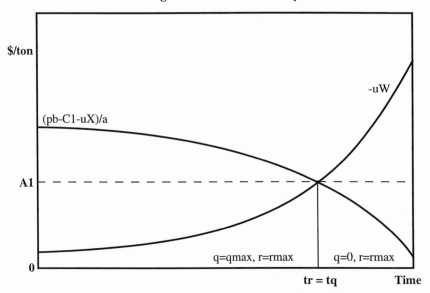

first subperiod, the problem is unconstrained.

Case three, $t_q < t_r$: This case has three subperiods as does case one (figure 4-3). The first and third subperiods have the same control and state variable behavior as in case one, but in case three there is a second subperiod between them where $r = 0$ and $q = 0$. During this second subperiod the waste pile decreases because its equation of motion becomes

$$\dot{W} = -kW \tag{22}$$

Therefore, if the waste pile remains below the critical level in the first subperiod, the constraint will never be active. Thus we have only two constrained solutions to consider, depending on whether the constraint becomes binding in the first or second subperiod. In the application in the next section, only the first constrained solution is pertinent; therefore the second solution will not be considered further.

The optimal behavior of the control variables can be summarized as follows:

$$q = \begin{cases} q_{max} & 0 \leq t \leq t_c \\ q_c & t_c \leq t \leq T \end{cases} \tag{23}$$

$$r = \begin{cases} 0 & 0 \leq t \leq t_c \\ r_c & t_c \leq t \leq T \end{cases} \tag{24}$$

The constrained levels of extraction and reclamation are selected to satisfy the necessary conditions within the limits of installed capital as discussed in the appendix:

$$q_c = \min\left\{ q_{max}, \frac{kW_c + r_{max}}{a} \right\} , \quad r_c = \min\{aq_{max} - KW_c, r_{max}\} \tag{25}$$

State variable behavior is given by the following equations:

$$X(t) = \begin{cases} X_0 - q_{max}t & 0 \leq t \leq t_c \\ X(t_c) - q_c t & t_c \leq t \leq T \end{cases} \tag{26}$$

Figure 4-3 Case Three: tr > tq

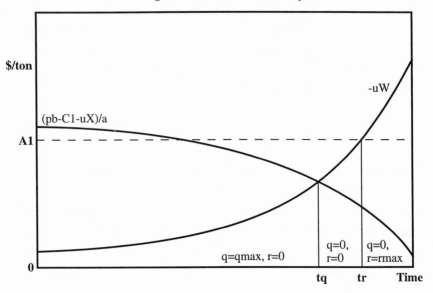

$$W(t) = \begin{cases} \dfrac{aq_{max}}{k} + \left(W_0 - \dfrac{aq_{max}}{k} \right) e^{-kt} & 0 \le t \le t_c \\ W_c & t_c \le t \le T \end{cases} \qquad (27)$$

Where X_0 and W_0 are the initial mass of the orebody and waste pile.

The instant when the constraint becomes binding, t_c is:

$$t_c = \frac{1}{k} \ln \left(\frac{kW_0 - aq_{max}}{kW_c - aq_{max}} \right) \qquad (28)$$

Terminal time is determined from (25), (27), and the known value of X(T):

$$T = \frac{X_0 - X(t_c)}{q_{max}} + \frac{X(t_c) - X_T}{q_c} \qquad (29)$$

Case Study in Clearwater National Forest

The linear-cost-function version of the model will be applied to the pre-feasibility analysis of a small open-pit gold mine in northern Idaho. The site is part of a larger ecosystem project the U.S. Bureau of Mines began evaluating in 1993. The mine is hypothetical but representative of the type of mine likely to be affected by ecosystem based regulations in this region. The purpose of the analysis is to determine the impact various levels of water quality standards will have on mine profitability. Impacts will be considered for two cases. First, the impact on the required ore grade a mine would need to discover to make zero (economic) profits at various constraint levels. Second, the impact on the (economic) profits of existing mines at various constraint levels.

The hypothetical mine is a small open-pit gold mine using heap leaching to recover gold from ore[10]. Model parameters for this mine are listed in table 4-1[11]. The mine is assumed to be located on the western edge of the Clearwater National Forest. Metals from the waste pile are assumed to drain into Lolo Creek. To make the ecosystem constraint tractable, rainfall and stream flow are taken to be

---

[10]The details of the hypothetical mine were provided by the U.S. Bureau of Mines.

[11]It is not the purpose of this paper to determine these values. Each of these values could be questioned but all are typical for this type of mine.

constants based on data from the U.S.D.A. Forest Service. The constant fraction of waste pile mass that migrates into the stream as metallic cations is taken from research at the Bureau of Mines on sulfate release from iron-bearing ores. This is not the appropriate constant but is used as a proxy for the actual constant which is not currently known. Cost functions for extraction are taken from those used in the U.S. Bureau of Mines prefeasibility analysis (Camm, 1992). Reclamation cost functions are taken from the HEAPREC model [6]. Both extraction and reclamation cost functions are linear.

The impact on the required ore grade of changes in the constraint level can be determined by writing the expression for the mine's profits as the sum of two terms. The first term accounts for profits realized while the constraint is

Table 4-1
Parameter Values for Hypothetical Mine

Quantity	Symbol	Value
Maximum Extraction (short tons/year)	qmax	7.24×10^6
Maximum Reclamation (st/year)	rmax	2.00×10^6
Metal Migration Rate (mg/short ton/year)[*]	k	250
Stream Flow (liter/year)	S	1.95×10^{10}
Rain Fall (liter/year)	R	4.18×10^6
Tons Overburden/Ton Ore	a	3.4
Extraction Cost ($/ton)	C_1	9.60
Reclamation Cost ($/ton)	A_1	0.50
Fixed Costs ($)	$C_0 + A_0$	6.26×10^7

* from White and Jeffers (1992) metal release rates for sulfates in iron ore rock.

non-binding, the second accounts for profits when the constraint is binding:

$$
\pi = \int_0^{t_c(W_c)} e^{-\delta t}(pbq_{max} - C_1 q_{max})dt
$$
$$
+ \int_{t_c(W_c)}^{T(W_c)} e^{-\delta t}[pbq_c(W_c) - C_1 q_c(W_c) - A_1 r_c(W_c)]dt - (A_0 + C_0)
$$

(30)

where q_c and r_c refer to the optimal choices of q and r when the constraint is binding and the dependence of t_c, T, q_c, and r_c on W_c is stated explicitly.

If values are chosen for E_c, W_c can be computed from (2), t can be computed from (20), and T can be computed from (29). Then (30) can be integrated to give the following equation for profits:

$$\pi = \frac{(pb - C_1)q_{max}(1 - e^{-\delta t_c})}{\delta}$$
$$- \frac{[(pb - C_1)q_{max} - A_1 r_c](e^{-\delta t_c} - e^{-\delta T}) - \delta(A_0 + C_0)}{\delta} \tag{31}$$

The lowest acceptable ore grade; that is, the grade of ore that just sets the sum of discounted profits to zero, is of particular relevance in potential supply analysis since it determines the lowest grade that will be developed under existing policies. If the existing policies change, the change in minimum ore grades can be related by mineral deposit models to the proportion of national mineral wealth that is no longer economically feasible. Once E_c is chosen, (31) can be solved for the value of b that sets $\pi = 0$:

$$b_0 = \frac{\delta(A_0 + C_0) + C_1 q_{max}(1 - e^{-\delta t_c}) + (C_1 q_c + A_1 r_c)(e^{-\delta t_c} - e^{-\delta T})}{p[q_{max}(1 - e^{-\delta t_c}) + q_c(e^{-\delta t_c} - e^{-\delta T})]} \tag{32}$$

Equation (32) is the basis for figure 4-4. In figure 4-4, b is interpreted as a minimum ore grade since, as was mentioned above, at constant technology levels, differences in b are attributable to differences in ore grade. Figure 4-4 shows the minimum ore grade that must be discovered for each level of environmental constraint at various discount rates.

Figure 4-4 shows the impact of various ecosystem policies on potential mines. The impact is a function of the expected mineral commodity price (assumed constant) and the discount rate used by the mine manager. For example, with a limiting stream metal concentration of 0.05 mg/L, at \$300/oz and a discount rate of 15%, the mine manager would be interested in ore grades of 0.089 oz/ton and better. With a higher commodity price, say, \$350/oz, the mine manager would be interested in grades as low as 0.076 oz/ton. At \$300/oz and a higher discount rate, say, 20%, the mine manger is only interested in grades of 0.103 oz/ton or better.

Figure 4.4 Minimum Economical Ore Grade

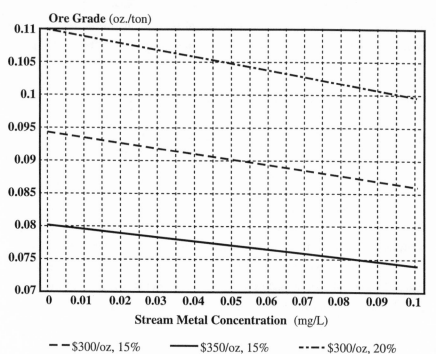

Figure 4-4 also shows the impact of policy changes on the development of the mineral wealth of a country. For example, at $300/oz and a discount rate of 20%, changing from 0.095 mg/L to 0.04 mg/L would require an increase in grade from 0.1 oz/ton to 0.105 oz/ton. Thus the exclusion of mineral deposits by policy changes can be quantified by the use of geostatistical inference about grade and tonnage relationships.

Using mineral deposit models changes in ore grades can be related to the tonnage excluded by such policies. For example if the deposit in this model is of the type that Cox and Singer (1986) identify as carbonate hosted gold-silver (model 26a, corresponding to disseminated deposits in the Carlin Trend of Nevada) then the shift from 0.100 troy ounces per ton to 0.105 troy ounces per ton in the preceding paragraph will eliminate about three percent of the occurrences of this type of deposit.

The impact of various policies on the level of economic profit at a particular mine can be determined by substituting (2), (12), and equation (33) (from the appendix) into (31). The resulting expression gives profits as a function of the limiting amount of metal in the stream (figure 4-5). For this figure the mine is assumed to already have found a deposit with an ore grade of 0.04 oz per ton.

Figure 4-5 shows profits increasing at a slightly decreasing rate as the allowable level of stream metal concentration is increased from 0 to 0.1 mg/L. Even at a tolerance of 0 mg/L, the mine is profitable--it earns discounted profits of slightly over 2.5 million dollars. This is entirely due to the initial assumption about finding a deposit with an ore grade of 0.04 oz./ton. The decrease in profits between any two points on the graph is the rent lost to a particular mine from increasing the level of ecosystem protection (decreasing the allowable level of effluent).

Conclusions

The model developed here shows a simple method for including ecosystem constraints into the framework of the Clean Water Act. The two key simplifying assumptions were ignoring ecosystem interactions across media borders so only aquatic effects were important, and concentrating on a simple one-way ecosystem effect in the aquatic food chain. For the simple economic model presented here, this abstraction is valid for most policy applications. Indeed, for most water policy matters, the model presented above is a valid synthesis of economic and environmental concerns. The special one-way relationship presented

Figure 4.5 Profits at Various Constraint Levels

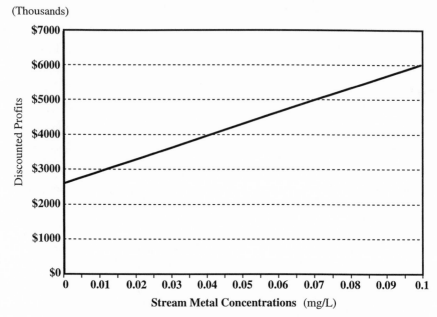

in this model is probably not valid for other media, where more complex relationships exist. The constraint here is certainly not optimal since it cannot be used to evaluate interspecies trade-offs nor does it account for stochastic utility that society might realize from certain species (for example, certain species might suddenly become valuable as sources for pharmaceutical). The constraint also greatly increases the required amount of information the policy maker needs to evaluate. Instead of setting effluent limits on an industry-by-industry and chemical-by-chemical basis, ecosystem standards would require site-by-site information as well. This additional information represents a significant increase in the cost of policy implementation.

The discussion of ecosystem constraints was set in the context of the behavior of a profit-maximizing mine manager facing an ecosystem constraint as well as the traditional depletion constraint. Obviously, the discussion is perfectly general and applies to firms in other industries as well. The mining framework points out the issues in the context of nonreplenishable resources and ties into some current policy issues. The interaction between the level of reclamation and production is important not only for the mine manager but also for policymakers. A mine manager is concerned with the impact of regulations on the profitability of a particular property, whereas, a policymaker is interested in the impact of a particular regulation on the level of mining activity in order to comply with the economic analysis requirements of Executive Order 12866. As the case study demonstrates, given the necessary information, the cost associated with a particular environmental standard can easily be estimated.

The cost of a policy change has two impacts. The first impact creates a barrier to entry for new mines by increasing the grade of ore the new mine must discover in order to be profitable. The second impact reduces the level of profits realized at existing mines. Both impacts provide incentives for mining firms to locate in places with less stringent environmental constraints. These incentives would have be weighed against a host of other factors the firm considers which are beyond the scope of this paper.

Another finding of the model of interest to both mine managers and policymakers concerns the life of the mine. If reclamation is undertaken prior to the waste pile reaching it's critical size, then the life of the mine will be shorter than the unconstrained case in extant literature. However, if reclamation is not undertaken until the constraint becomes binding, the life of the mine may be lengthened. An interesting extension of the model would be to incorporate other policy tools to evaluate the affect they would have on the mine life and tradeoff between ecosystem health and economic development.

Appendix - The Argument for Remaining on the State-Space Boundary

The first point to note is that the mine gets no reward for any environmental slack left in stock at the terminal time. The second point comes from considering the following example. Suppose q_{max} units of ore remain at t_c. Would it be more profitable to extract it all in the next period and adjust reclamation to ensure the waste pile stayed at the critical level or to let the waste pile fall below the critical level by deferring the extraction of some of the remaining ore? If it turns out to be more profitable to defer extraction, what is the optimal amount to defer?

First, calculate the profits the mine earns from staying on the state-space boundary (i.e., maintaining W at W_c) by extracting q_{max} and setting r as determined from (13):

$$r_c = aq_{max} - kW_c \tag{33}$$

With these choices, the following period would be the terminal period, T, and the mine would realize the following profits while the constraint is active:

$$\pi_1 = (pb - C_1)q_{max} - A_1(aq_{max} - kW_c) \tag{34}$$

Next, determine the profits if the mine retreats from the state space boundary by n units. Assuming the mine still sets reclamation as in equation (24) but defers production by n units for one period, then profits are

$$\pi_2 = (pb - C_1)(q_{max} - n) - A_1(aq_{max} - kW_c) + \left(\frac{n(pb - C_1)}{(1 + \delta)} \right) \tag{35}$$

No reclamation is necessary in the final period since the environmental slack created by retreating from the state-space boundary in the previous period, T-1, is exactly sufficient to cover the slack consumed by extraction in T. The difference between the profits realized by staying on the boundary and retreating are

$$\pi_1 - \pi_2 = \frac{\delta}{1 + \delta}(pb - C_1)n \tag{36}$$

The difference in profits is positive for all positive values of n. Therefore, it is never profitable to retreat from the state-space boundary. Furthermore, profits are maximized by always extracting the maximum amount (i.e., set q as large as possible and adjust r to make (13) zero when $W = W_c$).

The above argument for setting $q = q_{max}$ and $r = \underset{\sim}{r}$ as defined in (13) implicitly assumes $r_c < r_{max}$. If $r_c > r_{max}$, then r should be set at r_{max} and q should be set at q_c as defined below:

$$q_c = \frac{r_{max} + kW_c}{a} \tag{37}$$

References

Burness, H.S. 1976. "On the Taxation of Nonreplenishable Natural Resources," *Journal of Environmental Economics And Management* 3:289-311.

Camm, T.W. 1992. U.S. Bureau of Mines Information Circular 9298: Simplified Prefeasibility Cost Models for Mineral Evaluations Washington DC: GPO.

Conrad, Jon M. and Colin W. Clark 1987. *Natural Resource Economics: Notes and Problems*, Cambridge University Press, New York.

Cox, D.P. and D.A. Singer, eds. 1986. U.S. Geological Survey Bulletin 1693: Mineral Deposit Models Washington, DC: GPO.

Denton, D.K., S.R. Iverson, and B.B. Gosling 1992. U.S. Bureau of Mines Information Circular 9328: HEAPREC A Method for Determining Cyanide Heap Leach Reclamation Performance Bonds Washington, DC: GPO.

Forster, B.A. 1980. "Optimal Energy Use in a Polluted Environment," *Journal of Environmental Economics and Management* 7:321-333.

Hotelling, H. 1931. "The Economics of Exhaustible Resources," *Journal of Political Economy* 39:137-75.

Pindyck, R.S. 1982. "Jointly Produced Exhaustible Resources," *Journal of Environmental Economics and Management* 9:291-303 (1982).

Roan, P.F. and W.E. Martin, 1996. "Optimal Reduction and Reclamation at a Mine Site with an Ecosystem Constraint," *Journal of Environmental Economics and Management*, 30: 186-98.

Scott, A.T. 1967. "The Theory of the Mine Under Conditions of Certainty," in *Extraction, Resources and Taxation* Mason Gaffney, ed.

Seierstad, A. and K. Sydsaeter 1987. *Optimal Control Theory with Economic Applications* Amsterdam: North-Holland.

Vatin, A. and D.W. Bromley, 1994. "Choices without Prices without Apologies," *Journal of Environmental Economics and Management* 26:129-148.

White, W.W. and T.H. Jeffers, 1992. "Chemical Predictive Modelling of Acid Mine Drainage from Metallic Sulfide-Bearing Waste Rock," Proceedings of the American Chemical Society National Meeting, Washington, D.C.,

United States Environmental Protection Agency 1986 Statistical Analysis of Mining Waste Sample Data. Washington, D.C.: GPO.

Chapter 5
Costs and Benefits of Coke Oven Emission Controls

Timothy J. Considine
Graham A. Davis
Donita Marakovits

Introduction

Under Title III of the Clean Air Act Amendments, the US federal government is required to establish emission standards for coke oven batteries. Most existing methods of producing coke generate fugitive emissions that contain potentially carcinogenic substances, such as benzene soluble organics (BSOs). A variety of strategies, some entailing additional investment or higher operating costs, can reduce these emissions.

Several recent studies have estimated these costs with a static view of the industry. In contrast, this study considers plant closure decisions and new technology adoption. Furthermore, we estimate the potential health benefits from controlling coke oven emissions. Even though there is no requirement under Title III to examine benefits, such a task is important for broader public policy considerations. For instance, to what extent and at what cost is public health improved by cleaning up coke ovens? What are the orders of magnitude? Do we avoid 10 annual cancer cases for every million dollars spent or for every 100 million dollars spent? How certain are we of these estimates? These questions are the principal focus of this study.

Cancer incidence from pollution depends upon several complex relationships involving the transmission of hazardous substances through the atmosphere and the exposure of individuals to these substances. In addition, the probability of developing cancer from exposure to some specified amount of pollution is subject to considerable dispute. Cancer incidence also would depend upon not only the enforced emission levels but also upon how many and which domestic coke plants remain operating. Firms could shutdown existing ovens and import coke, thus, limiting domestic coke oven emissions by transferring the emissions abroad.

World coke supplies, however, are subject to the vagaries of international political events and economic conditions. Uncertainties on the costs and performance of new less toxic technologies also generate substantial risk. Since the behavioral reactions to regulations are subject to these uncertainties, then so too are the costs and benefits. Accordingly, we conduct a stochastic cost-benefit analysis of coke oven emission controls. We identify several critical economic and epidemiological parameters and then randomly sample from their probability distributions in calculating the costs and benefits of the proposed regulations.

At the core of our calculations is an engineering-economic model of the steel production process. The model is a linear program minimizing steel industry costs by selecting production and investment activities that satisfy a number of market and non-market constraints. This approach is necessary because the net cost of operating coke ovens depends upon the cost of direct inputs, such as coal and labor, and upon the implicit value of exhaust gases used to fire blast furnaces or to cogenerate electricity. In addition, this framework allows us to explicitly consider new production technologies, such as non-recovery coke ovens, along with other production options, such as retrofitting existing ovens to meet tougher environmental standards. Entry and exit decisions by individual producers can affect industry marginal abatement costs. Hence, we model these strategic options at the plant level.

We organize this paper as follows. The regulatory options and emission control technologies are discussed first, followed by a discussion of the process model and the calculation of annual cancer incidence. We then discuss the probability distributions used for the stochastic sensitivity analysis and present costs and benefits of alternative emission control policies. We finish by drawing some conclusions and by suggesting some policy implications.

Coke Oven Emission Controls and Technology

Most coke is produced by integrated steel companies using a process that applies heat to transform coal into a light porous material. Imports and U.S. merchant coking plants constitute the remaining sources of coke supply. The predominant method of producing coke in the U.S. is a wet coal charged process that produces relatively large amounts of residual off-gases that are distilled into by-products, such as petrochemicals, and/or utilized as fuel in downstream processes, such as in iron-making.

Given that the pressure within these ovens is relatively high, the lids and doors on coke ovens tend to leak unless they are hermetically sealed. Emissions also occur during the "charging" or loading of coal into ovens. In addition, exhaust gases can escape into the atmosphere via leaks at the lids and off-takes. Given these different emission points and the fact that no two coke oven batteries are exactly the same, measuring emissions from coke ovens is at best an inexact science.

Accordingly, pollution from coke ovens is not expressed in terms of some physical quantity, such as tons, but in terms of occurrences. For instance, door leaks are measured by observing the percentage of doors in a coke oven battery that are leaking over some time interval. Most existing batteries have limits set by state implementation plans that are generally consistent with the EPA's Reasonably Available Control Technology (RACT) limits under the National Emission Standards for Hazardous Air Pollutants (NESHAP) (see Table 5-1).

The EPA must issue emission control standards based upon a Maximum Achievable Control Technology (MACT) for all batteries. These standards are scheduled to be proposed by December 31, 1995. Another set of standards based upon a Lowest Achievable Emission Rate (LAER) are scheduled for implementation on January 1, 1998 for operators who seek more time to meet possibly even tougher future standards based upon risks to human health. The MACT and LAER standards involve limits placed on charging time and the allowable percentage of leaking doors, lids, and off-takes at coke batteries (see Table 5-1).

Besides importing coke or semi-finished steel, steel producers have essentially five technological options for complying with coke oven emission

Table 5-1
Comparison of Coke Oven Emission Standards

Emission Points	Emission Standards		
	Existing*	MACT	LAER
Doors (% leaking) (PLD)	10.7		
Tall		6.0	4.3
Short		5.5	3.8
Lids (% Leaking) (PDL)	3.2	0.6	0.4
Off-Takes (% Leaking)(PLO)	8.0	3.0	2.5
Charging (seconds per charge)	21.2	12.0	12.0

* Averages of limits that vary by plant

regulations: using sodium silicate luting compounds to plug leaks, retrofitting existing ovens, totally rebuilding coke ovens, adopting new coke oven technology, or adopting new coke-saving production technologies. The technical effectiveness as well as the costs and benefits of these strategies will vary for each establishment with the economic age of its coke oven batteries and blast furnaces.

Of the four emission points discussed above, doors are the single largest source of leaks. As Graham and Holtgrave (1990) point out, substantial progress has been made in reducing emissions from lids and off-takes and during charging. Although tar buildup and spring loaded hinges on doors tend to prevent leaks, coke oven doors often warp when they are opened as the extremely hot inside of the door is exposed to much cooler air outside the oven.

One technique to control leaks from these warped doors is to apply a sealant to the doors, such as sodium silicate. Several producers apply this material directly to their doors to prevent leaks. Once applied, the sodium silicate turns to a hard ceramic material. After continued use, the applications build up and become difficult to remove from the doors and jams. As a result, maintenance costs increase. Another problem is that use of sodium silicate voids door warranties and tends to mask door warpage and other problems that need repair. Given these and other problems, Environmental Quality Management, Inc., in a study for the American Iron and Steel Institute (AISI), concluded that the use of sodium silicate is not a viable long-term solution for controlling door leaks. Their analysis indicates that controlling door leaks is highly site specific and involves many factors including equipment, operation and maintenance, and managerial vigilance.

Given the thermal stress on doors, their environmental performance may decline with age. As a result, several integrated steel producers continuously repair and replace their coke oven doors. The cost and technical effectiveness of door and jamb replacements have been examined by the EPA and recently by the AISI. This information is incorporated into the process model discussed below.

The Amendments to the Clean Air Act also mandate an analysis of the Jewell version of the Thompson non-recovery coke oven. This design is similar to the obsolete Beehive coke ovens in which combustion of the coal gases occurs inside the oven. As a result, the controlled burning of the coal destroys the benzene soluble organics (BSOs) and other carcinogenic compounds contained in the off-gases. The waste heat from these gases can be used to produce steam for electricity generation. This technology has been characterized as "non-polluting" because there are no leaks as with conventional wet-coking ovens. There are, however, relatively large amounts of sulfur dioxide emissions that must be mitigated.[1]

Finally, there are several new iron and steel making technologies that could either substantially reduce or eliminate coking coal consumption. The first technique involves injecting crushed coal directly into a blast furnace. This pulverized coal injection (PCI) technology is used in Europe and Japan and is now being used on a limited scale in the United States. In addition, several technologies could completely replace coke plants in integrated iron and steel facilities. First, scrap-based steelmaking or so called "minimill" technology has been and continues to be a cost-effective way to bypass the coke and iron-making steps in steel production. Direct reduction, which has been in use for some time in areas with very limited scrap supplies and inexpensive natural gas, is another option.

In addition, there is the Corex process used in South Africa. This iron making technology essentially combines coal and iron in a smelter gasifer employing a fluidized bed reactor design that can utilize a relatively wide range of coals. Since the coking material is manufactured directly in the blast furnace, emissions of toxic substances are minimal. Finally, there is direct steel making that could eliminate the need for coke making in traditional integrated steel production. Unlike PCI, direct reduction, and Corex, this technology is currently not under commercial development. The U.S. Department of Energy and the AISI currently have a joint research project to build a prototype that is slated for completion in 1995. This technology has gathered considerable international attention, particularly in Japan, but is not considered in this study.

The adoption of these technologies depends upon several economic and engineering parameters, including relative material prices, capital costs and process yields. We develop an estimate of the likelihood of steel producers adopting these new technologies from our stochastic sensitivity analysis below.

The Process Model

Integrated steel production basically involves four steps: raw material preparation including coke production and iron ore preparation, iron making in blast furnaces, steel making using either pig iron or scrap, and finishing steel into final product shapes. In addition to providing material for iron making, coke plants indirectly provide energy for the rest of the steel plant. For instance, coke oven

---

[1]The only Jewell coke oven battery in the U.S. is a merchant coking operation at the mouth of a coal mine in Vansant, Virginia.

off-gases are often recycled to blast furnaces, to steel finishing operations, or to cogeneration plants. Calculating the implicit value of these off-gases is difficult because the value depends upon the purchased input prices and technical efficiencies at each point of off-gas generation and utilization. Simple applications of avoided cost using the price of natural gas do not adequately capture these interactions.

A common approach to this problem is to use a linear programming model as in previous studies of steel manufacturing conducted by Tsao and Day (1970), Russell and Vaughan (1976), and more recently by Sparrow, Farhangi, and McKinzie (1984). Tsao and Day specified a relatively small LP model in order to represent total industry input use and costs. Russell and Vaughan (1976) develop a much larger and more complex LP to estimate the costs of air and water pollution control for steel production. Unlike Russell and Vaughan's model, however, the model developed by Sparrow, which is largely based upon the technical input data from the Russell and Vaughan study, is smaller and, therefore, easier to verify.

We have extensively redefined and updated these models based upon current industry practices and upon recent information published in the technical literature. Furthermore, we have included the steel making technologies discussed above but not currently used in the United States. These technologies are included to permit an *ex ante* analysis of options for steel making under various policy regimes.

The model treats the United States steel industry as a combination of two plants, integrated mills and mini-mills. The integrated mills (SIC 3312-1) are "fully integrated", consisting of raw material preparation plants, coke ovens, blast furnaces, steel furnaces, and rolling and finishing mills. The mini-mills (SIC 3312-4) are representative of "partially integrated" mills without blast furnaces. Capacities available in non-integrated works and in steel finishing industries 3315, 3316, and 3317 are also included. The model allows the production of seventeen carbon steel products in three classes: 1) heavy structurals and rails, 2) plates, forms, and other slab-based products, and 3) bars, light structurals, and other billet-based products.

Total costs are the sum of variable input costs and capital charges for new investments and retrofits less credits for by-product sales. Total costs are minimized subject to five sets of constraints:

- plant material balances for each commodity that ensure shipments and external purchases are at least as large as the plant's requirements of each commodity,

- equipment capacity constraints including coke plant capacities that diminish over time based upon projected lifetimes,
- coke oven emission constraints that vary by policy scenario,
- market demand constraints that guarantee final product demands are met by the sum of the individual plants' outputs, and
- physical constraints on new capacity that limit annual equipment acquisitions to 10 percent of existing capacity and to 1 million tons for new equipment.

This last constraint is included because there is limited capacity of engineering firms to install new coking or Corex capacity in any one year.

Production is allocated assuming that each type of steel producer coordinates available plant capacities to utilize the optimal technologies first, and intermediate material flows are assumed transferable between processes with no transportation cost. For example, off-gas produced from coking activities within integrated steel mills is available for use at the blast furnace, and scrap produced in the finishing stages is available as an input to the steel-making process. Scrap is the only intermediate product allowed to flow between mini-mills and integrated mills at marginal cost.

This formulation of the model is not considered overly restrictive. First, the use of toll processing by many steel producers, in which a steel firm contracts with a lower cost producer to carry out certain steel manufacturing steps, does imply that "best" technologies are utilized before suboptimal ones. Second, steel production operations that produce valuable by-products tend to be situated near those steel manufacturing plants that consume such products. Nevertheless, the model should be seen as a "best case" production process, where all producers cooperate in planning technology utilization and intermediate product distribution. We have placed no lower constraints on equipment utilization, which would force suboptimal processes into use.

The model also includes equations that compute total cancer incidence. Our model is calibrated to previous estimates of cancer incidence using the Industrial Source Complex Model, which is a large and complex dispersion model. We assume that the average number of people exposed to coke oven emissions does not vary. However, we do allow cancer incidence to vary endogenously with the number of plants estimated to be operating in any one year or policy scenario. Annual cancer incidence for each plant is the product of four factors:

- the risk of getting cancer per unit of emissions,
- mean exposures per unit of BSO emissions, varying by plant,
- average percent leaking doors that vary by plant as well as by policy

scenario, and

- emissions of BSO per percent leaking door that also vary by plant and under the baseline, MACT, and LAER scenarios.

The mean value of unit risk is taken to be 6.2×10^{-4}, which is the same rate used in prior studies. The second factor can be interpreted as total exposure averaged over relatively small numbers of individuals that are exposed to high doses and a very large number of people that are exposed to minuscule amounts. The average percent leaking door data are from the 1992 cost study conducted by EPA. The emission rates are specified as an exponential function of leaking doors, which is the same functional form used in the 1987 EPA report.

Input Parameter Distributions

The stochastic sensitivity analysis starts with the quantification of uncertainty by specifying probability distributions for certain input parameters. We have utilized either historical data or prior studies to justify our judgments. The eight random input parameters, their distributions, and the characteristics of their density functions are summarized in Table 5-2.

The first major source of uncertainty concerns the amount of coke imports that can be purchased by the U.S. steel industry before world capacity constraints are reached and imported coke prices begin to rise. We have an upward sloping coke import supply function in the model but the size of the elastic portion over which large changes in imports could occur with very little change in prices is not really known. Based upon historical data on coke imports we have found that 5 million tons of coke imports appears to be a likely point at which coke import prices would began to rise. Accordingly, we take this as the mean position of the coke import supply function. Based upon our judgment that the odds of excess world coking supply above and below this amount are equally likely, we assume a normal distribution with a rather wide standard deviation of 2.1 million tons and a range that can span from zero to 12 million tons.

Next, since meeting the regulations involves investment, we consider the average cost of capital as a stochastic parameter. Here too we assume normality for similar reasons and use a mean estimate of 10 percent, which is derived from recent EPA costing studies. We use a rather wide range because some firms face very high rates of capital due to financial problems while others face relatively low rates.

Table 5-2
Input Parameter Distributions

Random Variate	Distribution	Mean	Standard Deviation	Range
Elastic Coke Imports (m tpy)	Normal	5	2.1	0 - 12
Cost of Capital (%)	Normal	10	2.0	6 - 18
Jewell Capital Cost ($/t)	Triangle	173	NA	160 - 325
Corex Capital Cost ($/t)	Triangle	250	NA	225 - 450
Coal Injection (t/thm)	Triangle	0.12	NA	0.12 - 0.25
Natural Gas Prices ($/mmbtu)	Normal	2.80	0.35	1.90 - 3.80
Steel Production (m tpy)	Normal	86.6	8.66	60 - 112
Unit Risk (Prob)	Weibull	6.2E-4	NA	1.3E-8 - 1.3E-3

The average capital costs for Jewell and Corex are taken from estimates supplied by their developers. Given the distinct possibility of cost over-runs, we assume a triangular distribution that is skewed to the high end. Triangular distributions are commonly used in cost-engineering studies (Dowlatabadi & Toman 1991; Humphreys 1984). Our conversations with several coke plant engineers indicated that there could be design problems involved with fitting a Jewell plant into an integrated steel facility. For Corex there are substantialuncertainties concerning the scaling up of this process to replace the relatively larger blast furnaces.

Based upon engineering studies, the pulverized coal injection rates can vary between 0.12 and 0.25 tons of coal per ton of hot metal. We adopt the low end as the mean to be conservative but allow a triangular distribution to acknowledge the claims by many engineers that these rates can be increased substantially.

Natural gas prices are varied because coke oven gas, despite its low heat content, is a substitute for natural gas used to fire boilers, furnaces, and other equipment. Hence the price of natural gas affects the value of coke plant off-gases. Gas prices can vary widely by season and with secular trends in the industry. The distribution specified above is based upon the range of variation for industrial gas prices over the past 5 years.

Domestic steel production also can vary considerably due to variations in steel imports and in apparent steel consumption in the U.S. The standard deviation for steel production is based upon the last five years of experience while the range is based upon a much longer historical record that spans 1950 to 1990.

Finally, a Weibull distribution is assumed for unit risk (EPA, 1987). The range of variation in this parameter is huge, spanning at the high end a one in one thousand chance of getting cancer from 1 milligram of BSO per cubic meter to a low end estimate of 1 in 100 million chance of developing cancer.

These probability distributions are assumed to be independent because these parameters involve separate aspects of the planning problems facing steel producers. For example, the amount of excess world coking capacity is probably unrelated to U.S. steel production. Latin Hypercube sampling is used to sample from the distributions. We generate 100 random experiments for each of the eight parameters to cover the full range of the probability density functions.

Estimates of the Stochastic Costs and Benefits

The linear programming model is run with these random variates to generate probability distributions for the endogenous variables in the process model, such as cancer incidence, production costs, investment, and coke imports. The model is run with and without the MACT emission standards in 1995 and with and without the LAER emission standards in 1998 for a total of 400 model solutions.

There is also a dynamic aspect of the model. A substantial portion of wet coking capacity is expected to be economically obsolete over the next 10 years. To capture this natural attrition we "age" wet coking capacities assuming a 40 year life for coke oven batteries. For instance, from 1992 to 1995, domestic wet coke making capacity is expected to decline by 3.2 million tpy, or 13.2%, due to natural attrition. By 1998, wet coking capacity is expected to decline by 5.5 million tpy, or by 22.7%. Rather than specifying a multi-period linear programming problem, we reduce computational requirements by selecting 1995 and 1998 as base years and adjust the investment constraints to allow for the passage of time. So in 1995, the industry would have 4 years of investment and 7 years in 1998. Under the policy scenarios, we then compare the structure of the industry with and without emission standards at these two points in the future: in 1995 for MACT and in 1998 for LAER.

Under the 1995 and 1998 base runs, declining domestic coke capacity is accommodated through a combination of reduced coke demand in steelmaking, additional coke imports, and investments in new coking capacity. Coke consumed by the steel industry is estimated to decline roughly 6.4% by 1998 due to cost-effective replacement of traditional blast-furnace based iron making with other processes that eliminate the need for coke within integrated mills. For example, investments in the Corex process (1.3 million tpy of capacity) and electric arc steel making (8.2 million tpy of capacity) from 1992 to 1998 are estimated to reduce total annual steel making costs compared to current practice.[2]

Given coke imports in the $95.00 to $100.00 per ton range, mean coke imports are estimated to be more than 6 million tons per year in 1995 (see Table 5-3). This rise in coke imports above current levels not only replaces expiring domestic ovens, but also replaces coke production from the higher cost U.S. wet-coke producers who are forced to shut down due to the availability of low cost imports. This result, however, is knife-edge, depending on the assumed price of coke imports. A coke import price beginning at $98.00 reduces the import level to around 2 million tons per year, which is closer to present levels, and fewer domestic shutdowns occur. Hence, we cannot be confident in the 1995 base case level of domestic wet-coking production and coke imports. However, the standard deviations around the import estimate do reflect this degree of uncertainty, and should be kept in mind as an important outcome of the analysis.

Under the 1998 base case, coke imports decline slightly from the 1995 base, to 5.8 million tons per year as further investments in Jewell coking capacity displace declining wet-coking production and imports (see Table 5-3). These base cases show that coke imports and investments in Jewell and Corex allow the U.S. steel industry to adjust relatively painlessly to the aging of domestic wet coking capacity.

---

[2]Bearing out our forecasts, Geneva Steel is currently considering investment in the Corex process to replace dated blast furnaces in the production of iron.

The imposition of MACT in 1995 causes only minor changes in coke markets and in the steel industry. Coke consumption declines by an additional 150,000 tons per year due to increased investment in Jewell and Corex. Coke imports rise by 240,000 tons (see Table 5-4). These adjustments keep the increase in total industry annual costs to $9 million (see Table 5-5), which is considerably below the $25 to $33 million estimated recently by the standards development branch of EPA. The reason for our lower estimate is that we allow the industry to select new production technologies and to import coke. This allows a significant amount of old wet coking capacity to be retired in the base case, thereby, reducing the number of plants that must be retrofit to meet MACT.

Annual cancer incidence drops from an estimated 1.1 cases in the base

Table 5-3

Baseline Projections of Coke Supply and Demand

	Million Tons Per Year Standard Deviation	
	1995	1998
Coke Demand	19.92(1.20)	18.86 (1.08)
Domestic Coke Production	13.89(1.61)	13.18 (1.98)
Old Coking Production	11.79 (1.58)	10.11 (1.82)
New Coking Production (Jewell)	2.10 (1.91)	3.07 (2.95)
Coke Imports	6.02 (1.96)	5.67 (2.04)

Table 5-4
Estimated Average Coke Market
Adjustments Under MACT

	Million Tons per Year Standard Deviation
Coke Demand	
Coke Consumption under Base Case (1995)	19.92(1.200)
Reduction in Coke Consumption Under MACT	0.20
Coke Consumption Under MACT (1995)	19.72 (1.228)
Coke Supply	
Domestic Production Compliance Ovens	0.65 (0.000)
New Capacity Additions	2.19 (1.890)
Retrofitting Noncompliance Ovens	10.70 (1.524)
Total Domestic Production	13.54
Coke Imports	6.18 (1.94)
Coke Supply	19.72

Table 5-5
Comparison of Base Case and MACT Averages in 1995

	Base	MACT	% Change
Total Variable Costs (billions $)	25.017 (0.062)	25.026 (0.062)	0.04%
Employment (mill/man-hrs/yr)			
Coke Plants	11.026 (1.192)	10.727 (1.125)	-2.71%
Other	231.184 (3.550)	230.500 (3.626)	-2.71%
Total	242.211	241.23	-2.71%
Annual Energy Purchases			
Electricity (mill MWH)	26.261 (0.311)	26.258 (0.279)	0.01%
Natural Gas (trill BTU)	275.890 (51.993)	275.391 (51.703)	0.18%
Residual Oil (trill BTU)	116.225 (1.890)	116.112 (33.140)	0.10%
Distillate Oil (trill BTU)	41.296 (1.197)	41.295 (1.191)	0.005
Annual Materials			
Coal (mill t)	26.198 (2.607)	25.651 (2.594)	-2.09%
Iron Ore Materials (mill t)	67.988 (2.472)	67.510 (2.549)	-0.70%
Scrap (mill t)	47.179 (0.440)	47.106 (0.417)	-0.15%

Table 5-5 (Cont.)

	Base	MACT	% Change
Capital Expenditures (bill $) ('92-'95)			
Coke Oven Retrofits	0.00 (0.000)	0.023 (0.010)	-
New Coke Ovens	0.458 (0.398)	0.478 (0.393)	4.37%
New Blast Furnances	0.301 (0.441)	0.312 (0.449)	3.65%
Steel Furnances	0.692 (0.007)	0.693 (0.005)	0.14%
Continous Castings	0.082 (.181)	0.083 (0.180)	1.22%
.. Total	1.533	1.589	3.5%
Cancer Incidence (cases)	1.089 (0.571)	0.494 (0.272)	-59.5

Table 5-6
Estimated Average Coke Market Adjustments Under LAER

	Million Tons per Year Standard Deviation
Coke Demand	
Coke Consumption under Base Case (1995)	18.86(1.081)
Reduction in Coke Consumption Under LAER	0.46
Coke Consumption Under LAER (1998)	18.40 (1.221)
Coke Supply	
Domestic Production Compliance Ovens	0.64(0.086)
New Capacity Additions	4.25 (3..023)
Retrofitting Noncompliance Ovens	7.37 (2.271)
Total Domestic Production	12.26
Coke Imports	6.13 (2.041)
Coke Supply	18.40

Table 5-7
Comparison of Base Case and LAER Averages in 1998

	Base	LAER	% Change
Total Variable Costs (billions $)	24.986 (0.062)	25.006 (0.063)	0.08%
Employment (mill/man-hrs/yr)			
Coke Plants	10.156 (1.138)	8.936 (1.404)	-12.01%
Other	230.854 (3.496)	229.945 (3.824)	-0.37%
Total	241.010	238.881	-0.88%
Annual Energy Purchases			
Electricity (mill MWH)	27.535 (0.327)	27.591 (0.351)	0.20%
Natural Gas (trill BTU)	273.414 (53.625)	272.304 (53.269)	-0.41%
Residual Oil (trill BTU)	116.225 (34.095)	116.604 (33.900)	-0.30%
Distillate Oil (trill BTU)	41.582 (1.084)	41.576 (1.115)	-0.01%
Annual Materials			
Coal (mill t)	24.971 (3.228)	23.804 (3.444)	-4.65%
Iron Ore Materials (mill t)	64.997 (2.505)	64.393 (2.808)	-0.93%
Scrap (mill t)	47.179 (0.440)	47.106 (0.417)	-0.18%

Table 5-7 (Cont.)

	Base	LAER	% Change
Capital Expenditures (bill $) ('92-'95)			
Coke Oven Retrofits	0.00	0.023	-
	(0.000)	(0.010)	
New Coke Ovens	0.458	0.478	4.37%
	(0.398)	(0.393)	
New Blast Furnances	0.301	0.312	3.65%
	(0.441)	(0.449)	
Steel Furnances	0.692	0.693	0.14%
	(0.007)	(0.005)	
Continuous Castings	0.082	0.083	1.22%
	(.181)	(0.180)	
.. Total	1.533	1.589	3.5%
Cancer Incidence (cases)	1.089	0.494	-59.5
	(0.571)	(0.272)	

case to 0.5 cases under the MACT standards. The results indicate that each avoided cancer case is expected to cost on average about $15 million.

The estimated cost and market impacts of the LAER standards are larger than those estimated to occur under MACT. Coke consumption declines by almost one half million tons (see Table 5-6) due to additional investment in Corex and Jewell. Coke imports rise from the base case. In addition, almost one million extra tons of Jewell coking capacity is estimated to be installed.

Annual cancer incidence drops from an estimated 1.075 cases in 1998 to 0.341 cases under the LAER standards. So going from MACT to LAER yields a 0.179 reduction in cancer incidence. The reason for this finding is that emission rates are exponential functions of door leaks down to about a 2 percent leaking door limit. After that the functions become almost linear. So as regulation squeezes out the last remaining door leaks the marginal increment to health diminishes. This lower benefit yield dramatically raises the unit cost of LAER to an average of $30 million dollars per avoided cancer case.

Conclusions and Suggestions for Further Research

The approach developed in this study may be valuable for other cost-benefit studies of toxic waste regulation. Process modeling permits an informative description of industry cost structures and the likely responses to regulation. Conducting stochastic sensitivity analysis with process models could be useful in risk assessment. The analysis presented above could be improved by exploring the coke import question in more depth and by applying statistical measures to summarize the results from the stochastic sensitivity analysis. Finally, more flexible forms of regulation, such as exposure trading, should be examined. The large differences in population densities around coke plants in the US suggest that compliance costs can be significantly reduced with exposure trading.

References

Environmental Protection Agency (1987). Coke Oven Emissions from Wet-Coal Charged By-Product Coke Oven Batteries: Background Information and Proposed Standards, Office of Air Quality and Standards, Research Triangle Park, N.C., EPA-450/3-85-020a.

Environmental Quality Management, Inc. (1991). Survey and Evaluation of Coke Oven Door Sealing Practices, prepared for the American Iron and Steel Institute, Cincinnati, Ohio.

Dowlatabadi, Hadi and M.A. Toman (1991). Technology Options for Electricity Generation, Baltimore: Johns Hopkins University Press.

Graham, John D. and D.R. Holtgrave (1990). "Coke Oven Emissions: A Case Study of Technology-Based Regulation," *Risk-Issues in Health & Safety*, Summer, 243-272.

Humphreys, Kenneth K., ed. (1984). Project and Cost Engineers Handbook, New York: Marcel Dekker, Inc.

Russell, C. and W. Vaughan (1976), Steel Production: Processes, Products, and Residuals, Baltimore: Johns Hopkins University Press.

Sparrow, F., A. Farhangi, and L. Mckinzie (1989), Indiana State Utility Forecasting Group Least Cost Utility Planning Model, The Iron and Steel Industry, Natural Resources Research Institute, Purdue University.

Tsao, C.S. and R.H. Day (1971), "A Process Model of the US Steel Industry," *Management Science*, Vol. 17, No. 1, B588-B608.

Chapter 6
Modeling Equilibria and Risk under Global Environmental Constraints

Alain Haurie
Richard Loulou

Introduction

Policy makers are consistently in need of technical analysis to support decision making. This is particularly true in the environmental area due to the variety of paradigms that must be integrated to analyze the regulatory options. The aim of this paper is to assess the contribution of optimization based applied systems analysis models in the understanding of complex interrelations between the economy, energy and the global environment. Recent concerns about global environmental changes associated with energy production and use raise a whole list of policy issues such as:

- the search of synergetic effects in pollution abatement techniques;
- the management of risk;
- the allocation of costs among different regions;
- the negotiation of international cooperation agreement, etc.

Applied systems analysis methods contribute to policy analysis by allowing the simulation of detailed scenarios. This methodology takes into account a large number of interactions between different economic agents and/or techno-economic modules. Our claim is that a Mathematical Programming framework provides a good tradeoff between three important objectives, namely

- a sufficiently detailed representation of the fundamental techno-economic options,
- a coherent representation of the economic processes underlying energy use, and
- a good tractability of the simulations or scenario generator.

The paper is organized in three sections examining three important features of the interactions between economy, energy and the environment which are:

- *Market Equilibrium* paradigm, where the energy choices of the agents are dictated by an underlying optimization by each agent;
- *Game Theory* aspect of international or interregional negotiation and cooperation; and

- *Decision in Uncertainty* paradigm involved in many investment and production activities.

Each section concludes with an assessment of the fulfilment of the three criteria listed above by Mathematical Programming systems analytic models.

Computing economic equilibria

One cornerstone of applied economic theory is the *Supply-Demand Equilibrium* paradigm. The equilibrium is the intersection of an upward sloping *supply curve* of the production sector and a downward sloping *demand curve* of the consumption side. The supply and the demand curves are the result of a profit maximizing behavior of the producing firms, and utility maximizing behavior of the consumers. In the description of the energy system of a region, there are many goods, represented by different energy forms, and many competitive uses of the energy forms by the consumers of energy services. The computation of an equilibrium is therefore a nontrivial task. In the following subsections we shall investigate different mathematical programming approaches for the computation of supply-demand equilibria in energy models.

The energy supply function

We first concentrate on the description of the energy production system under environmental constraints.

The energy production model

In a competitive market, the output of a profit maximizing firm producing a single good will be at a level where the *marginal cost* is equal to the price of the good. Therefore the supply curve is also the *marginal cost curve*. Mathematical programming models produce very efficient estimates of the marginal costs. They are the *shadow prices* of the *demand constraints* in a cost minimizing model. Therefore the first building block of an energy model is a representation of the production processes with the costs involved. The system's cost minimization, under demand satisfaction constraints, provides the supply curve of the energy supply sector.

In order to represent correctly the fundamental ingredients of the total system's cost one has to introduce:

1. a time horizon $\{t = 1, \ldots, T\}$;
2. a list of *technologies* $\{j = 1, \ldots, n\}$ and for each technology j a list of three

(interrelated) activities:
- *investment* or *capacity increase*, denoted $y_j(t)$;
- *production* or *capacity utilization*, denoted $x_j(t)$;
- *installed capacity*, denoted $z_j(t)$;

3. a list of *energy carriers* $\{I = 1, \ldots, p\}$ which correspond to the various semi-finished products and energy forms that are the inputs and outputs of the technologies.
4. a set of exogenous *demands* $\{d_i(t): I = 1, \ldots, m\}$ to be satisfied by the system.

The production side model can therefore be summarized by the following mathematical programming problem which, for simplicity and tractability, is formulated as a *Linear Program* (LP).

$$\min \sum_{t=1}^{T} \beta^t \sum_{j=1}^{n} [cinv_j(t)y_j(t) + cop_j(t)x_j(t) + cmain_j(t)z_j(t)] \qquad (1)$$

s.t.

$$z_j(t) + \sum_{r=1}^{t} A_j(\tau)y_j(\tau) = resid(t), \quad t=1, \ldots, T; \; j=1, \ldots n \qquad (2)$$

$$B(t) \begin{bmatrix} y(t) \\ x(t) \\ z(t) \end{bmatrix} \leq 0, \; t=1, \ldots, T \qquad (3)$$

$$\sum_{j=1}^{n} D_{ij}(t)x_j(t) = d_i(t), \; t=1, \ldots, T; \; i=1, \ldots m \qquad (4)$$

In this formulation the cost criterion (1) is the sum over time, and over all technologies, of the investment (cinv), operations (cop), and maintenance (cmain) discounted costs (with discount factor β). In these costs are included the energy imports costs and energy exports revenues. The constraints (2) represent the capacity transfers over time, given the residual capacities and the life durations of each technology. The constraints (3) represent the various bounds on utilization, investment, installed capacities, for each technology, as well as the energy carrier balance equations. Finally the constraints (4) represent the exogenous demands (e.g. final energy) to satisfy.

Global environmental constraints

The energy system is also contributing to the emission of a set of pollutants $\{l = 1,..., p\}$. We thus add to the model (1) - (4) a set of constraints

$$\sum_{j=1}^{n} E_{lj}(t)x_j(t) \leq e_l(t), \ l=, \ . \ . \ . \ , p, \tag{5}$$

where $E_{lj}(t)$ is the emission coefficient of technology j for pollutant l at time t and $e_l(t)$ is the imposed *global constraint* on emissions of type l at time t.

The *shadow prices* $v_l(t)$ of these environmental constraints represent the marginal system costs for satisfying at time t the emission standards. They also give an indication of the correct *emission tax* which should be levied in order to induce the energy producer to observe this global constraint. The latter assertion is true in view of a fundamental duality result of mathematical programming (Luenberger, (1973)).

Market allocation with inelastic energy service demands

In this subsection we consider a particularly important class of models where the market equilibrium can be simulated via a single criterion optimization. We show that this is a direct consequence of an assumption of price inelastic demand for energy services. We then consider some important applications made within this particular framework.

A single optimization equilibrium model

The demand for the *final energy forms* is a *derived demand*. Basically there exist demands for a whole list of *energy services* such as *residential heat, commercial heat, industrial outputs, various kinds of transportation services, etc.* These demands are also often called *useful energy demands*, a term which is somewhat misleading since these demands are not always expressed in energy units. The consumer of an energy service utilizes *end use* or *demand technologies* to `transform" some energy carriers into the required service. Given a list of technology choices and a price for each energy carrier, the *final energy demand* derived from an exogenous demand for energy services is represented as the result of a cost minimization mathematical programming problem.

If the energy carriers are priced at the marginal production cost defined in the previous section, and if the demand for energy services is exogenous,∴ demand does not change with the price of energy, then a well known property of duality in linear programming (Dantzig, 1963), the *supply-demand equilibrium for final energy* is obtained as the solution of a single enlarged linear program where the demand constraints express the demand for energy services and the technology list includes also the end use devices. Therefore, under these limiting assumptions of price-inelastic demands for energy services and marginal cost pricing of energy carriers, a single LP run finds a supply-demand equilibrium!

This is the approach of several comprehensive energy models developed in the last decade or so. The most typical of these models is MARKAL, whose acronym means *MARket ALlocation*, and which has been developed by ETSAP, a consortium of several Organization for Economic Cooperation Development (OECD) nations. A detailed documentation of this model can be found in Fishbone and Abilock, (1981) and Berger, *et al.*. (1992). A MARKAL model gives a coherent description of the substitution effect among different final energy forms resulting from changes in the prices (i.e. the marginal costs) of these energy carriers. Typical applications of MARKAL are reported in Wene and Ryden, (1988), Berger, *et al.*, (1991b), and Baillard-Haurie, *et al.*, (1987).

Assessing marginal costs of CO_2 emission abatement in Quebec and Ontario

MARKAL models of the energy systems in Quebec and Ontario have been developed and used to evaluate the respective costs of reducing CO_2 emissions in accordance with Toronto and IPCC guidelines. Results of these simulations have been reported in Loulou and Waaub, (1992). In each case, particular attention has been devoted to the representation of energy intensive industrial sectors. Also, an oil refinery submodel allows a representation of the long term adjustment of this sector to changes in the consumption patterns of refined products (e.g. switches to lighter products).

In Tables 6-1 and 6-2 we show the total discounted cost increase for each province, due to the satisfaction of the CO_2 abatement constraints over the time horizon 1990-2030.

Table 6-1
CO_2 abatement costs for Quebec (CDN 1980 M$)

CO_2 Abatement	High Growth		Moratorium		Low Growth	
none		0		110		0
constant	10520	(.36%)	12452	(.43%)	1783	(.07%)
10%	13276	(.46%)	15952	(.55%)	3162	(.12%)
20%	16226	(.56%)	19672	(.68%)	5220	(.20%)
35%	20975	(.72%)	25659	(.88%)	9482	(.35%)
50%	26183	(.90%)	32204	(1.1%)	14574	(.55%)

Table 6-2
CO_2 abatement costs for Ontario (CDN 1980 M$)

CO_2 Abatement	High Growth		Low Growth	
none		0		0
constant	51208	(.88%)	22410	(.42%)
10%	60760	(1.04%)	29172	(.55%)
20%	71420	(1.23%)	37394	(.71%)
35%	95112	(1.63%)	51480	(.97%)

In Figures 6-1 and 6-2 we summarize the marginal cost evaluation for these two provinces, as computed by MARKAL. Two remarks can be immediately made about these results. First, there is an important difference between the two provinces both for total and for marginal costs. This discrepancy shows that two neighboring regions can have very different technological options for CO_2 abatement.

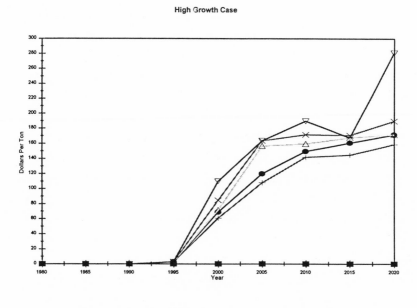

Figure 6-1 CO$_2$ Abatement Marginal Cost for Québec

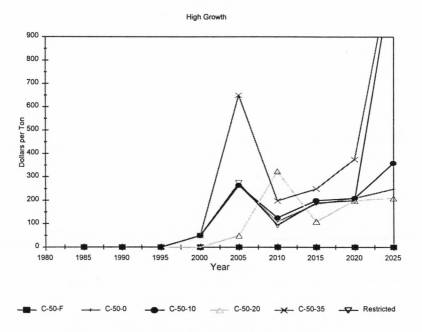

Figure 6-2 CO$_2$ Abatement Marginal Cost for Ontario

Second, the underlying economic assumption of marginal cost pricing of final energy forms is not realistic. However, in this assessment of the relative costs for regions, this perfect market assumption provides a *benchmark* which permits the analyst to eliminate the spurious influences of already existing energy taxes and other market distortions.

Assessment of the contribution to problem understanding

We now turn to assessing the performance of the MARKAL approach with respect to the three criteria proposed in the introduction. production and end-use processes. For example, The Quebec MARKAL data base the industrial subsectors it is possible to represent many current and future contains more than 500 technologies. The only limitation is really the availability of reliable data. Therefore the representation of the techno-economic options is very good. With this level of technology detail the model can detect the synergetic effects in productivity and emission reductions.

Economic coherence: Paradoxically, the weakness of MARKAL is that it has too strong an economic consistency. As already indicated, the marginal cost pricing, implicitly assumed in running the model, does not correspond to the existing energy markets where electricity is often priced at average cost and oil products like gasoline can have up to 75% of their price due to taxes. Therefore the simulations obtained cannot be taken as predictions of actual market behavior. However when the policy analysis issue is technology assessment, as in the CO_2 abatement case, the strong economic consistency of MARKAL is valuable in that it provides benchmark situations, and sets socially desirable goals for policy makers.

Tractability: MARKAL is a highly tractable model. Recent hardware and software advances in personal computers and workstations have considerably reduced the run times for the generation of a set of scenarios. A dedicated data base support system, called MUSS (Goldstein, 1991), allows the user to build and maintain a complex techno-economic data base with a minimum effort.

The case of explicit demand laws for final energy forms

In this subsection we consider the computation or simulation of market equilibria when the energy demand is specified through explicit demand laws. Such laws may be obtained via econometric analysis.

Equilibrium computation `a la PIES

For some problems the detailed description of the end use technology choices is not essential or is not accessible. The final energy demand is then described through an explicit demand law which associates with a set of prices a set of final energy demands. The computation of a supply-demand equilibrium where the supply function is determined as the marginal cost schedule of a production model and the demand law is explicit (e.g. obtained through econometric estimation), has been implemented in the *PIES* model. A proof of convergence of the algorithm has been given in Hogan and Weyant, (1983). The basic idea can be summarized as follows: Let, for a single good, $P_s(q)$ and $P_d(q)$ be the (inverse) supply and demand curves respectively. Introduce for any $Q > 0$ the functions:

$$F(Q) = \int_0^Q P_s(q)dq \qquad\qquad (6)$$

$$G(Q) = \int_0^Q P_d(q)dq \qquad\qquad (7)$$

Under general conditions the equilibrium is defined by the value Q* which maximizes the difference:

$$H(Q) = F(Q) - G(Q) \qquad\qquad (8)$$

In a multi-commodity context the analog of the function *F(Q)* is not defined when there are nonsymmetric cross elasticities. However in Hogan and Weyant, (1983), it is shown that convergence is also obtained if one neglects locally the cross elasticity effects, thus working with a *relaxed demand schedule*, and proceeding with a sequence of approximate equilibria involving updated relaxed demand schedules.

Regulated equilibria

The *PIES* algorithm computes a partial economic equilibrium where the pricing of goods is at marginal cost. As we know, many energy markets are regulated (e.g. through monopoly of utilities or through taxation). It has been shown in Hogan and Weyant, (1983) that via a simple scheme which consists in adding some appropriately defined delivery costs for the regulated energy forms, one can adapt the *PIES* algorithm so that it computes an equilibrium with regulated prices.

In Berger, *et al.,* (1987), an energy supply model for Quebec, consisting of a MARKAL model restricted to the production of final energy forms, has been coupled with a demand function derived from a comprehensive demand simulation model, called MEDEQ (see Pellegrin, 1984). This coupling has shown the tractability of the method.

The case of implicit demand laws for final energy forms

A supply-demand decomposition technique

In the previous section we have shown how the law of demand for a final energy form could be implicitly defined by an optimization model. If we have a multi-regional or a multi-sectoral model with a high level of detail in the description of each region or sector, then the overall supply/demand model may be too large for attempting a direct optimization approach. In that case one may attempt implementing a decomposition technique which is similar in spirit to the *PIES,* algorithm where, at each step, one uses a local approximation of the supply and demand schedules. Contrary to *PIES* however, the demand schedule derived from an optimization model is not explicitly available, but is rather the implicit *value function* of the demand side linear program, parametrized on the demand vector. The local approximation for such a demand function can be derived through *sensitivity analysis* performed on the consumption submodel. Here again, in the price information exchange, may introduce various price regulations and therefore mimic imperfect markets. This approach is described in Loulou, *et al.,* (1993), where the producer is the electricity producer for Quebec and the consumer is the rest of the energy system of the province. The heuristic decomposition can be schematically described as follows:

Initialization $k: = 1, \ d^k: = 0$

> Step 1: Compute a local approximation $Z^k(\cdot)$ of the inverse demand function, via sensitivity analysis performed on the demand vector of the consumers LP around the current demand d^k

Step 2:   Compute a tentative equilibrium by solving the following LP:

$$Min \; X,d \; cX \; -Z^k(d)$$
$$s.t. \; AX \; - \; d \; \geq \; 0 \quad\quad\quad\quad (9)$$
$$X \in L_1$$

Step 3:   Let d^{k+1} be the optimal solution obtained at step 2. If $d^{k+1} = d^k$
then STOP; otherwise set k: = k+1 and GOTO **Step 2**.

Note that at step 2 the supplier uses its own complete linear program to compute a cooperative equilibrium between the exact supply curve and the approximate demand curve. Although there is no complete formal proof of convergence, the method has successfully converged toward the global optimum in all instances, in some cases thanks to additional relaxation steps. Table 6-3 summarizes the convergence of a typical instance of the Quebec Supply/Demand decomposition experiment.

Table 6-3
Performance of the supply-demand decomposition algorithm

Decomposed Model	Iteration 1	Iteration 2	Iteration 3	Iteration 4	Total
Supply Model	1725 p.	2256 p.	52 p.	684 p.	4717 p.
Demand Model	7594 p.	804 p.	378 p.	39 p.	8815 p.
Convergence Gap	104103	949	654	0	
CPU time (min)	23.3	8.4	5.9	6.4	44.0
Global Model					18488 p.
CPU time (min)					55.6

* p. Stands for pivots

Assessment of the contribution to problem understanding

Level of detail: The supply-demand decomposition technique allows the highest level of detail for the description of each module in the multi-regional or multi-sectoral model. The only limit is the available knowledge of the technologies in each module.

Economic coherence: The supply-demand equilibrium paradigm is the *inference engine* in the scenario/simulation production. Furthermore, the possibility of representing taxes or other market regulations in the price setting process increases the realism of the simulation.

Tractability: This supply-demand decomposition technique has not proved to converge in all cases. In particular, the discontinuous implicit supply and demand schedules prevent it from always converging. However, as indicated in many experiments reported in Loulou, *et al.*, (1993) convergence or approximate convergence is obtained in most cases. The method is also implementable for more than two sectors or regions.

Multi-agent interactions, negotiations and cooperation

Economic equilibria described above rest on the assumption that supply and demand functions (be they explicit or implicit) are well defined, and that the decisions of the various economic agents are governed by these functions. For instance, economic theory tells us that when perfect competition prevails, the implicit pricing mechanism is that of marginal cost, with the consequence that the competitive equilibrium is also a cooperative equilibrium. Some situations do not satisfy these assumptions, for instance when a monopolistic (or oligopolistic) supply side is not or insufficiently regulated. In such situations, the noncooperative aspect of the transaction must be dealt with explicitly, and this is the realm of (noncooperative) Game Theory. We shall examine two types of noncooperative games corresponding to the Nash equilibrium and Stackelberg solution concept respectively.

Competitive Nash equilibria

A Nash equilibrium with n players is a set of decisions x_i, $I = 1, \ldots, n$ such that when any n-1 decisions $x_1, \ldots, x_{k-1}, x_{k+1}, \ldots, x_n$ are fixed, the remaining player's decision x_k maximizes that player's profit. In some cases involving the trading of commodities, a Nash equilibrium does not exist. For instance, a game with one supplier, one consumer and one commodity, where the supplier is free to fix the price and the consumer is free to fix the amount purchased, does not have a Nash equilibrium, since once a quantity has been chosen by the consumer, the supplier can increase its price indefinitely in order to maximize its profit. On the other hand, if the supply and demand sides are represented by a supply and a demand curve respectively, the Nash equilibrium is precisely the supply-demand equilibrium described previously.

In energy-environment modeling, interesting Nash equilibria can be defined when certain special rules determine the way prices are set. For instance, the regulations regarding the trading of electricity between a utility and independent producers operating in a given state or country. Haurie, *et al.*, (1992) examines the case of New England and the PURPA rule stipulating that *the utility must buy electricity from co-generators at the utility's marginal cost.*

In the other direction, the utility generally sells electricity at its average production cost. Note that this rule differs from marginal cost pricing in two respects: first, the utility sells at average cost, and second, it buys at *its* marginal cost, rather than at the co-generator's marginal cost as would be the case in a pure marginal cost pricing scheme. A special algorithm was devised, which resembles somewhat the decomposition scheme described above, and which allowed the computation of a Nash equilibrium. The algorithm goes as follows:

Initialization: Choose initial vector s^0 of quantities of electricity purchased by the cogenerators. Set $k = 0$.

Step 1:   Solve the utilities Linear Program and compute its average electricity cost. Then, using parametric analysis, compute an approximate marginal cost function in the vicinity of s^k. This function is separable and piece-wise constant.

Step 2:   Solve a tentative equilibrium problem by allowing the co-generators to buy electricity at the utility's average cost, and to sell electricity along the marginal cost function computed at step 1. This computation involves an expanded linear program.

Step 3:   STOP if $s^k = s^{k-1}$, ELSE let $k = k+1$, and GOTO Step 1.

The above algorithm converged quite rapidly on a realistically sized model of the New England situation.

Table 6-4 outlines the main differences between three types of solutions; the cooperative optimum, the status quo (no cogeneration), and the Nash equilibrium under PURPA. One observes that the cost of the PURPA solution exceeds that of the cooperative solution, but is lower than the total cost under the *status quo* and that the co-generators derive a significant cost advantage from PURPA, at the expense of the utility, which sees its cost increase. Note also that the PURPA solution shows much increased electricity sales by the co-generators compared to the cooperative solution, whereas in the *status quo*, co-generators

Table 6-4
Comparison of three equilibria between Utility and
Co-generators

	Total Cost (US 1980 M$)			Average Cost of Electricity (Mils/Kwh)			Electricity Purchased (Twh)		
	COOP	Status Quo	PURPA	COOP	Status Quo	PURPA	COOP	Status Quo	PURPA
Utility	7196.1	7154.2	7219.4	-	63.39	64.61	5.965	0	8.192
Co-generator	1070.7	1160.0	1061.4	-	89.03	81.47	0	0.946	0
Total	8266.7	8314.2	8280.8	66.16	66.54	66.28	-	-	-

purchase a modest amount from the utility. Another consequence of the PURPA rule is to increase by 2% the average cost of electricity sold by the utility.

Stackelberg equilibria

In a Stackelberg equilibrium, one player is assumed to be a *leader* that makes an unchallenged decision and announces it. All other players are *followers* who maximize their profits, knowing the leader's decision. Of course, in making its decision, the leader anticipates reactions of the followers. One example of a Stackelberg situation arises when there are two producers of a certain commodity, one major and one minor. The major producer (leader) announces a capacity increase decision, and the minor producer then adjusts its own production level knowing the leader's capacity.

Another typical situation arises when a monopolistic leader is in the position of setting the price of a commodity, and the consumers adjust their purchases (and perhaps other decisions as well so as to minimize their costs. In the latter type of situation, the leader is also called the *price setter* and the followers are *price takers*. In Savard, *et al.*, (1993), a utility is assumed to act as a monopolistic leader that fixes electricity prices, while consumers (followers) have the option of substituting other energy forms and conservation, if they wish. The utility anticipates the reaction curves of the consumers before setting the prices. The Stackelberg Equilibrium problem is formulated as a *Bi-Level Programming Problem* as follows:

$$Min \; cY + PQ$$
$$Q$$
$$s.t. \; BY + Q \geq b \qquad \qquad \textbf{(10)}$$
$$Y \in L_2$$

and Q is the solution of:

$$Max \; PQ - cX$$
$$Q$$
$$s.t. \; AX \geq Q \qquad \qquad \textbf{(11)}$$
$$X \in L_1$$

where P, Q are respectively the price and quantity vectors of electricity sold, X is a vector of activity variables by the utility, and Y is a set of activity variables by the consumers. There is a hierarchy of decisions in the above formulation, whereby the second level (the follower's) optimization can be solved for each fixed value P, yielding a purchase decision $Q(P)$, whereas the upper level optimization is solved fully knowing the follower's reaction rule $Q(P)$.[1]

In the particular case just described, we have devised an *ad hoc* algorithm (Savard and Loulou, 1993) and applied it to the case of the Quebec energy system, over a 20 year horizon divided into 4 periods of 5 years. Each period is further divided into six time divisions (3 seasons times 2 diurnal divisions), yielding a commodity vector of dimension 24. The gist of the approach consists in decomposing the optimization into a) the computation of an *approximate* reaction rule $Q'(P)$ for the follower, and b) the solution of the leader's optimization problem in which the approximate reaction rule has been explicitly injected, as sketched below.

Initialization: $k: = 1$

      Step 1:   Compute an approximate reaction curve $Q^k(P)$.

      Step 2:   Solve the leader's problem:

---

[1] Bi-level programming is a recent and difficult branch of mathematical programming (see Bard and Falk, 1982; Bialas and Holmes).

$$Max \; cX \; - \; PQ^{k}(P)$$
$$Q$$
$$s.t. \; AX \; \geq \; Q^{k}(P) \tag{12}$$
$$X \in L_{1}$$

Step 3:   Let P^{k}, Q^{k} be the optimal solution obtained at step 2. If $Q^{k} = Q^{k-1}$
then STOP; otherwise set $k: = k+1$ and GOTO **Step 2**.

The choice of the approximation $Q^{k}(P)$ at each iteration is of course
crucial in insuring the success of the method. In Savard and Loulou, (1993) we
compute $Q^{k}(P)$ by using a local parametric analysis performed on the follower's
program, around the previous value P^{k-1} of P, and we obtain separable, piece-wise
constant demand curves. Although not guaranteed to converge to a global
Stackelberg equilibrium in all cases, the approach was observed to stop after a
small number of iterations (typically 15 to 25 for large problems), and the point
thus obtained is then easily seen to be at least a local Stackelberg equilibrium. In
table 6-5 below, we present the main results of this application, and compare them
to a cooperative solution. It is thus seen that the Stackelberg solution is (as
expected) much more favorable to the utility (which sees its total cost reduced
significantly), and much less favorable to the consumers, whose costs increase.
Globally, the total (utility plus consumers) cost in the Stackelberg solution exceeds
the cooperative total cost by about 8%.

Assessment of the contribution to problem understanding

Level of detail: Because each agent of the noncooperative games is
described via its own submodel, a high degree of disaggregation is possible. In this
respect, the models can be as detailed as those used in the more traditional
decomposed linear programs described previously.

Economic coherence: By allowing various behaviors by the players, the
noncooperative game models add considerably to the set of economic situations
that can be modeled formally.

Table 6-5
Comparison of the Stackelberg and Cooperative Equilibria
between Utility and Consumers

	Period	Cooperative Equilibrium	Stackelberg Equilibrium
Total Electricity Demand (Petajoules/ year)	1	125.4	119.1
	2	190.0	81.9
	3	194.5	91.6
	4	174.4	99.1
Electricity Prices (Cents/Kwh)	1	0.52	2.81 to 5.04
	2	0.52 to 1.29	2.01 to 9.05
	3	1.83	2.43 to 13.09
	4	2.23	2.55 to 13.44
Total Costs (Supply + Demand in M$)		38973	42121

Tractability: There are not yet general, reliable algorithm for the computation of Nash or Stackelberg equilibria, when each player is represented by a large mathematical program. The work reported here represents appreciable progress towards the practical resolution of such games. Its principal limitation is the lack of guarantee of convergence, which forces the modeler to use *ad hoc* convergence enhancement mechanisms in some instances. Of particular difficulty is the case of the Stackelberg equilibrium, since it is not amenable to convex programming, and therefore runs the risk of resulting in local rather than global solutions.

Fair sharing of cooperation dividends
There are numerous situations where several economic agents can derive substantial benefits from cooperation, and would be willing to share these benefits via compensation payments (side payments). In all such cases, a global optimization program which puts all resources in common yields a solution whose profit exceeds the sum of profits that the individual players (or indeed some sub-coalitions) of the players would be able to achieve. We propose to examine

some situations where cooperation has substantial advantages, and discuss ways to share these advantages between the different players.

Shapley values

A cooperative game between n players is likely to exist if any subcoalition S can "do better" than the same coalition minus one or more of its players. In other words, we look for situations where the *Characteristic function F(S)* is super-additive, i.e.

$$F(S + T) \geq F(S) + F(T) \tag{13}$$

where S and T are two disjoint subcoalitions of the n players, and the characteristic function $F(S)$ is the maximum benefit coalition S can achieve, if formed. Some authors define $F(S)$ as the maximum benefit coalition S can achieve *assuming that all other players play against coalition S*. Such a pessimistic viewpoint is not often relevant in economic applications and we shall simply assume that all players which are not part of coalition S are neutral. The super-additivity property of course entails that the maximum total benefit is always obtained by the grand coalition G of the n players. The central question of cooperative game theory is the fair sharing of the benefits obtained by the grand coalition among all players.

The Shapley Value (Shapley, 1953) proposes a unique sharing having the desirable property that the share of player I is commensurate with its power, (i.e. its ability to improve the benefits of a coalition which it joins). The Shapley value $v(I)$ for player I is given by:

$$v(i) = \sum_s \frac{(n-s)!(s-1)!}{n!} (F(S) - F(S -[i])), \ i \in G. \tag{14}$$

where the summation is performed on all coalitions $S \subseteq G$ that contain player I, while S-$[I]$ is coalition S minus player i, and s is the number of players in coalition S.

In Berger and Haurie, (1990), we examine the benefit derived from operating four electricity production systems in cooperation. The four regions of Quebec, Ontario, New York state, and New England are connected by electricity transport lines whose capacities may be increased via additional investments by the players concerned. Therefore, if coalition S forms, it can decide jointly whether to increase the capacities of the lines that link the members of that coalition. If no coalition forms, the current transmission capacities will continue to prevail in the future.

We built a four-region MARKAL model restricted to the electricity sectors only, and driven by exogenous electricity demands over the horizon 1990-2020. In order to do so, the MARKAL software was augmented to be able to distinguish several electricity grids within the same model (see Berger, *et al*, 1992). The model was then run as many times as there were viable coalitions. Table 6-6 shows the nine coalitions and the values of the total system cost for each coalition, taking the *status quo* (empty coalition) as the base case, with a cost arbitrarily set at zero. As can be seen, the total net benefit of the grand coalition is equal to 470.7 million dollars, whereas that of the Quebec-Ontario-New England coalition achieves a benefit of 398.13 million, etc. The imputations of the total benefits via Shapley value are shown in table 6-7. The shares attributed to Quebec and to New England are quite large because these two players contribute the most to any coalition which they join, as can be seen from table 6-6.

Finally, table 6-8 exhibits the capacity increase decisions adopted by the optimization of the grand coalition, showing that the Quebec-New England and the Ontario-New York links are the only two that should be significantly increased.

Trading energy and emission rights

In the case study just described, it has been possible to build a single MARKAL model encompassing all four players. Such a task is often cumbersome, or even impossible, when the individual systems are too large, or when there are many players. In such cases, it is necessary to implement methods for the derivation of the cooperative optimum of a coalition without running one large mathematical program encompassing all players. Above we have described a decomposition approach where separate supply and demand models of an energy system are *composed* so as to compute a global optimum. Similar approaches can be used for cooperative multi-regional energy exchanges, another very frequent situation. The decomposition of linear programs with special structure is a very active area of theoretical and algorithmic research (Goffin, *et al.,* 1992 and Goffin, *et al.,* 1993a). In contrast to these sophisticated approaches, Loulou and Waaub, (1992) use a simple *ad hoc* approach to compose the Quebec and Ontario MARKAL energy models under CO_2 emission constraints. Two types of cooperation are defined and treated, the first involving the efficient sharing of

Quebec Hydro electricity, and the second the efficient trading of CO_2 emission rights.

Table 6-6
Total benefits achieved by each coalition
(US 1980 M$)

Coalition	Benefits
Status Quo (empty coalition)	0.00
Québec - New York	22.64
Québec - New England	373.90
Québec - Ontario	19.83
Ontario - New York	70.58
Québec - New York - Ontario	110.41
Québec - New York - New England	373.90
Québec - Ontario - New England	398.13
Grand Coalition	470.70

Table 6-7
Benefit sharing using the Shapley Value
(US 1980 M\$)

Player	Allocated Benefit	Share
Québec	202.4	43.0%
New York	39.3	8.40%
New England	182.0	38.6%
Ontario	47.0	10.0%
Total	470.0	100.0%

Table 6-8
Transmission Lines Capacities in the Empty and the
Grand Coalitions (GW)

Coalition	Year	Status Quo Current Capacity	Grand Coalition Optimal Capacity
QC-NY	2000	2.18	2.18
	2005	2.18	2.18
		2.18	2.18
		2.18	2.18
		2.18	2.18
QC-NE	2000	2.20	2.20
	2005	2.20	3.26
	2010	2.20	5.35
	2015	2.20	6.20
	2020	2.20	6.20
QC-ON	2000	1.65	1.65
	2005	1.65	1.65
	2010	1.65	1.65
	2015	1.65	1.65
	2020	1.65	2.20
ON-NY	2000	2.15	2.15
	2005	2.15	2.15
	2010	2.15	3.84
	2015	2.15	5.36
	2020	2.15	5.36

- Efficient use of hydro-electricity: Each provincial model is run independently, with a preset emission limit (chosen as a constant CO_2 policy). The two models are run repeatedly, assuming each time that an amount X of Quebec hydro-electricity is *dedicated* to Ontario. The amount X is then varied from 0 to 14 Gigawatts, and the total costs of a constant CO_2 policy are recorded as shown in table 6-9. Note that the maximum joint benefit is obtained for a dedicated capacity of 14 GW, but that the marginal benefit of the last 3 GW is almost nil.

- In the same situation, another type of cooperation can be imagined, consisting of trading emission rights. In table 6-10, the costs of various CO_2 policies in the two provinces are computed in two different ways: first, it is assumed that each province must *independently* abate CO_2 by a preset percentage; the second method assumes that the two provinces jointly decide how much to abate each, while *globally* satisfying the preset CO_2 limit. Of course, the second method incurs less cost than the first, and the difference is the benefit of cooperation via emission rights trading. Note that this benefit is very low when the CO_2 constraint is mild, but rises to about 3 billion dollars for large CO_2 reductions. Table 6-11 complements the information in table 6-10 by showing the allocation of CO_2 emissions among the two provinces.

Assessment of the contribution to problem understanding

Level of detail and economic coherence: On these two dimensions, the use of fair sharing schemes certainly adds to the interest of computing cooperative equilibria. Even though perfect cooperation rarely exists in practice, the computation of such an idealized solution is useful in setting a benchmark which should be approached if not actually attained during the course of negotiating an agreement.

Tractability: The computation of Shapley values is in principle straightforward, but requires one run of a mathematical program for each viable coalition, and may thus become prohibitive if a large number of players are free to coalesce in any number. In practice however, much insight can be gained even with a limited number of judiciously selected coalitions. Another source of improvement of computational efficiency comes from the use of decomposition techniques to solve the mathematical programs representing coalitions. Such programs, by their very nature, are akin to multi-regional problems with a structure

Table 6-9
Joint cost savings as a function of electricity
trading between Quebec and Ontario
(CDN 1990 M$ discounted to 1990)

Electricity Traded	Cost Increase for Québec	Cost Decrease for Ontario	Net Savings
0 GW	0	0	0
3 GW	390	9436	9046
8 GW	1352	16603	15251
11 GW	1822	20850	19028
14 GW	2154	21504	19350

Table 6-10
CO_2 abatement costs with and without emission
rights trading (CDN 1990 G$)

Emission Abatement	Total Cost Without Emission Trading		Total Cost With Emission Trading		Net Benefits
	Québec	Ontario	Québec	Ontario	
None	0	0	0	0	0
Constant	6.73	35.92	6.92	33.74	0.002
10%	13.26	60.33	17.83	55.21	0.542
20%	15.97	72.71	23.86	63.46	1.367
35%	20.63	94.29	28.90	82.92	3.096

Table 6-11
Allocation of CO_2 emissions with and without emission rights trading (M tons/year)

Emission Abatement	Annual Emissions Without Trading		Annual Emissions With Trading	
	Québec	Ontario	Québec	Ontario
None	78.9	247.3	78.9	247.3
Constant	65.7	139.2	63.8	141.1
10%	64.0	133.6	61.0	136.3
20%	62.1	127.3	58.1	131.3
35%	59.3	118.6	55.0	122.9

appropriate for the usual decomposition schemes.

Decomposition techniques generally allow larger models to be solved, in less computer time. Great progress has been made in recent years, both on theoretical and algorithmic aspects of decomposition of structured linear programs. This progress has been aided by the increased speed and decreased cost of modern computers, to the point where quite large programs can now be entirely processed on modestly priced portable computers. The next step should be the commercial availability of production grade, efficient decomposition packages and their user friendly incorporation in existing large scale linear programming solvers.

Risk management

Energy systems are risk prone. Uncertainty prevails in many aspects including:

- Investment costs;
- availability of equipment;
- date of introduction of backstop technologies;
- world price of fossil fuels; and
- severity of the required pollution abatement.

These are just a few of the long list of uncertainties plaguing the policy analysis process. In this section we discuss the contribution of *dynamic and stochastic programming* methods in dealing with risk in policy analysis.

Random scenarios

Basically the uncertainty affecting the energy-environment system is described as a stochastic process $\xi(t)$ taking its values in a set E. This uncertainty may affect all the parameters of the activity analysis model. Thus we rewrite the production model (1)-(4) as follows:

$$\min \sum_{t=1}^{T} \beta^t \sum_{j=1}^{n} [cinv_j^{\xi(t)}(t)y_i(t) + cop_j^{\xi(t)}(t)x_j(t)$$
$$+ cmain_j^{\xi(t)}(t)z_j(t)] \tag{15}$$

s.t.

$$z_j(t) + \sum_{r=1}^{t} A_j^{\xi(t)}(t)y_i(\tau) = resid^{\xi(t)}(t),$$
$$t = 1, \ldots T; j = 1, \ldots n \tag{16}$$

$$B(t)^{\xi(t)}(t) \begin{bmatrix} y(t) \\ x(t) \\ z(t) \end{bmatrix} \leq 0, \ t=1, \ldots ,T \tag{17}$$

$$\sum_{j=1}^{n} D_{ij}^{\xi(t)}(t)x_j(t) = d_i^{\xi(t)}(t), t = 1, \ldots T; i = 1, \ldots m \tag{18}$$

Therefore we can have disturbances affecting the cost coefficient as well as the residual capacities or the technical coefficients and the final demands.

A dynamic programming-simulation framework

If the decisions taken by the economic agents are influencing the probability measure of the stochastic process $\xi(\cdot)$ then the only sensible way to try to optimize this system is to implement a *Dynamic Programming* approach. In the above model the state variable at period t, summarizing the past influences on the system, will be the pair $(z(t), \xi(t))$, where z is the vector of all installed capacities. Then the decision at period t, i.e. the activity levels $(I(t), y(t), x(t))$, will be adapted to the history of the $(z(\cdot), \xi(\cdot))$ process, (e.g. as a *feedback law*). It is well known that the computation of optimal feedback laws involves a dynamic programming approach which suffers the *curse of dimensionality*. It is therefore totally unrealistic to envisage to compute optimal strategies or feedback laws for a stochastic energy-environment model 'a la MARKAL.

A way to circumvent this difficulty is offered by a method consisting of

$$0 \quad \geq \quad G(s(t, \omega_n), \sigma(\theta, s(t, \omega_n))). \qquad (19)$$

to substitute a *parameter design* problem to the dynamic optimization problem. This idea has been exploited in large scale reservoir management models (see Breton, 1978). It proceeds by considering a family of strategies (feedback laws) indexed over a finite dimensional *parameter set* Θ. In order to simplify the notations let's call $u(t)$ the vector of all independent decision variables and $s(t) = (z(t), \xi(t))$ the state vector at time t. Denote $u(t) = \sigma(\theta, s(t)s$ as the strategy which corresponds to the choice of the parameter θ. The optimal design problem is then summarized as follows:

$$\min_{\theta \in \Theta, s(\cdot)} E[\sum_{t=0}^{T} \beta^t g(s(t), \sigma(\theta, s(t)))] \qquad (20)$$

s.t.

$$s(t + 1) \quad = \quad h(s(t), \sigma(\theta, s(t)), \quad t = 0, \ldots T \qquad (21)$$

$$0 \quad \geq \quad G(s(t), \sigma(\theta, s(t)). \qquad (22)$$

Let Ω denote the sample space for the $\xi(\cdot)$ process. A sample path is then the sequence $\{(z(t, \omega), \xi(t, \omega): t = 1, \ldots, T\}$. A sample of size N will consist in N sample paths $\{(z(t, \omega_n), \xi(t, \omega_n): t = 1, \ldots, T, n = 1, \ldots N\}$. Given such a sample we solve the following problem:

$$\min_{\theta \in \Theta, s(t,\omega_n), t=1,...T, n=1,...T} \frac{1}{N} \sum_{n=1}^{N} [\sum_{t=0}^{T} \beta^t g(s(t,\omega_n), \sigma(\theta, s(t,\omega_n))] \tag{23}$$

s.t.

$$s(t+1, \omega_N) = h(s(t,\omega_N), \sigma(\theta, s(t,\omega_N))), \quad t = 0, \ldots T, \tag{24}$$

$$0 \geq G(s(t,\omega_n), \sigma(\theta, s(t,\omega_n))). \tag{25}$$

This is now a standard mathematical programming problem. It has been shown in Robinstein (1986) that, under relatively general assumptions, the policy obtained in solving the system (23)-(25) converges almost surely, when the sample size N tends to ∞ to the solution of (20)-(22). Therefore, we can approximate an optimal dynamic programming policy in a given class indexed over a parameter set Θ via the solution of a large-scale standard mathematical programming problem.

A stochastic programming framework

When the perturbation process has a probability measure which is independent of the decisions then one can implement a more powerful technique called *stochastic programming*. In its simplest form the perturbation process $\xi(\cdot)$ is represented as an event tree describing the unfolding of the uncertainty over time. A path from the root to an extremity of the event tree represents a *scenario*. Each scenario has a given probability. At each node υ of the event tree is defined as a set of constraints and an economic function which involve variables specific to that node and also variables specific to the antecedent nodes (i.e. nodes on the path from the origin to node υ).

A *scenario* is defined as a path leading from the *root node* to a specific *terminal node*, it also corresponds to a *terminal node* of the event tree. In Rockafeller *et al.*, (1987) and Wets (1987) a *scenario aggregation* approach has been proposed for the solution of stochastic programming problems. This provides, at the same time, an implementable decomposition technique for solving the very large scale mathematical programming resulting from this event tree description of the dynamics and also a nice way to present the fundamental structure of the stochastic programming approach. In order to describe the method in simple terms consider the event tree shown in Fig. 6-3 with 12 nodes and 3 scenarios.

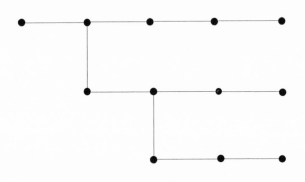

Figure 6-3
A Simple Event Tree

We also use a schematic description of the activity analysis model. Let S be the set of all possible scenarios, p_s the *weight* (or probability) given to scenario s, $x(s)$ the variables, C_s the constraint set, and $f(x(s), s)$ the cost criterion associated with scenario s.

Assume perfect foresight. Then one knows which scenario is realized. The optimization problem when one knows that scenario s is realized can be written

$$\min \quad f(x(s),s) \tag{26}$$

$$s.t.$$

$$x(s) \in C_s. \tag{27}$$

This problem is relatively small. We can solve such a problem for each scenario $s \in S$ and thus get a so-called *admissible perfect foresight strategy*:

$$x \doteq (x(s))_{s \in S} \doteq (x_1(s), \ldots, x_T(s)_{s \in S}), \tag{28}$$

where T is the time horizon of the model. Figure 6-4 illustrates this concept.

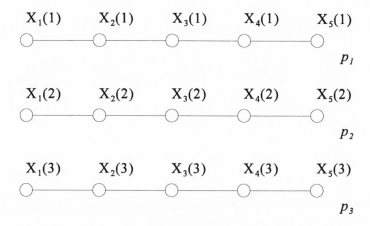

Figure 6-4
A Perfect Foresight Strategy

Since one generally does not have perfect foresight, the information unfolds progressively and two different scenarios s and s' may thus be indistinguishable up to time t. Therefore, it will be necessary to have, for these two scenarios, equality between the two streams of actions

$$x_t(s) \doteq x_1(s)), \ldots, x_T(s) = (x_t(s)) \doteq (x_t(s') \doteq$$
$$x_t(s'), \ldots, x_T(s')). \tag{29}$$

One says that a strategy x is *implementable* if it satisfies this condition for all pairs of scenarios that are indistinguishable up to time t, $t = 1, \ldots, T$. Let I be the set of all implementable strategies.

We can now write the problem as follows:

$$\min \sum_{s \in S} p_s f(x(s), s) \tag{30}$$

s.t.

$$x(s) \in C_s \ \forall s \in S \tag{31}$$

$$X \in I. \tag{32}$$

Therefore, a solution of the stochastic programming problem is a strategy which is both *admissible* and *implementable* and which minimizes the expected cost.

The approach proposed in Rockafellar and Wets, (1987); and Wets, (1987) builds sequentially admissible strategies and implementable strategies according to the following procedure:

1. **scenario aggregation:** Given an *admissible* strategy x^{v-1} construct an *implementable* strategy Figure 6-5.

2. **auxiliary perfect foresight problems**: For each $s \in S$ solve:

$$\min \ f^v(x(s), s) \tag{33}$$

s.t.

$$x(s) \in C_s \tag{34}$$

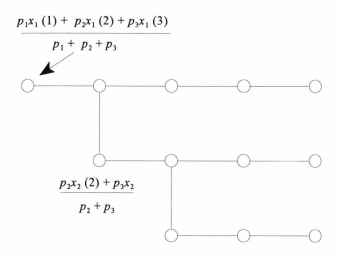

Figure 6-5
Averaging the Solution

where:

$$f_v(x(s),s) = f(x(s),s) + \sum_{t=0}^{T} [w_t^{v-1}(s)(x_t(s)$$

$$+ \frac{1}{2}\rho[x_t(s) - x_t^{v-1}(s)]^2]$$

(35)

Call the solution x^v.

3.   multiplier update:

$$w_t^v(s): = w_t^{v-1}(s) + \rho[x_t^v(s) - x_t^v(s)].$$

(36)

$v: = v + 1$ and repeat.

To be more precise in the definition of the averaging process we consider for each t the coarsest partition P_t of the set of scenarios S, such that if $A \in P_t$, and

$s,s' \in A$, the scenarios s and s' are indistinguishable up to time t. Therefore, an implementable strategy will be such that the decision variables at period t are identical for all scenarios in each set A of the partition P_t, for $t = 1, \ldots, T$. Given an admissible strategy x we get an implementable one by the following averaging process. For each $A \in P_t$, let:

$$p_A \doteq \sum_{s \in A} p_s, \tag{37}$$

and then define:

$$x_t(s) \doteq x_t(A) \; \frac{1}{p_A} \sum_{s \in A} p_s x_t(s). \tag{38}$$

There are other possible approaches for exploiting the particular structure of stochastic programming models. Particularly promising are those methods which implement a *column generation* technique in association with *interior point* algorithms (see Birge, Goffin, *et al.*, (1993).

Risk Management
The dynamic or stochastic programming approach permits the modeler to take risk into account in the analysis of possible policies. As in the classical literature in finance(Markowitz, 1959) it will be possible to derive efficient trade-off curves between minimum expected system cost and limited risk. We give below two typical examples where this risk management is important for energy models.

Risk Assessment in Hydropower Generation
Some countries (e.g. Colombia) have a rich endowment in water resources which permitted them to invest heavily in hydro generation systems. However, recent climatic changes have triggered long periods of low water inflows in the reservoirs with, as a result, a necessity to implement power rationing. An energy model for such a country should include a description of possible scenarios concerning the length of the dry periods. This would make the availability factors of the hydro equipment a random process. The investment decisions recommended by a stochastic programming model will be based on an efficient compromise

between the cheap expected cost of hydro power generation and the risk associated with possible low inflows. In particular *hedging* equipment, like fossil fuel plants could be incorporated in a diversified portfolio of equipment.

Buying Greenhouse Insurance

In a very interesting paper (Manne and Richels, 1991) the problem of the optimal reaction of a country like the USA, to the global warming threat has been posed as a *decision analysis problem*. The event tree describes the unfolding of uncertainty about the severity of the global warming phenomenon and the level of trace gases emission curbing which will be necessary to enforce. The risks are in this instance either to overreact or not to prepare enough for a necessary reconversion of the energy system. Actually the evaluation done in Manne and Richels involve a computable economic equilibrium model. Extending the approach to a more detailed description of the energy production and utilization system is one of the goals of the ETSAP committee which supervises the *MARKAL* developments.

Assessment of the contribution to problem understanding

Level of detail: The approaches described in this section permit the modeler to keep a very detailed description of technology and energy choices. The stochastic programming approach is the best known way to include risk assessment in dynamic choices.

Economic coherence: The stochastic programming method extends readily to the computation of market equilibria or Cournot-Nash equilibria. The strategies will be called *s-adapted* since, as indicated in Haurie, *et al.*, (1992), the decisions will be adapted to the sample path of the perturbation process $\xi(\cdot)$.

Tractability: The stochastic programming method requires very heavy computational efforts, since the size of the mathematic programming model is roughly multiplied by the number of nodes in the event tree. Recent advances in computer hardware and software and recent progresses in advanced implementation of decomposition technique have dramatically increased the tractability of these methods.

Conclusions

Mathematical programming models of the energy system have been first proposed in the 70's. The motivation for their development had been the oil crises and the need for OECD countries to identify alternative energy sources and new technologies to cope with a possible global scarcity or an unreliable supply of crude oil. Lower world prices for oil have reduced the need to find new energy sources. However, increased concerns about the environmental consequences of energy production and use are again on the forefront of energy policies for developed as well as developing nations. More than ever one needs to evaluate the implicit costs of various energy options. We must also evaluate the implied economic cost of imposing global emission constraints on the energy system. This is a necessity either in a *command and control* approach or if one prefers to implement *market based* instruments to reach global environmental objectives. In the first case one must identify the technology options to promote through legislation and controls. In the second case one must have a first guess of the effluent taxes or of the tradeable emission permit prices in order to avoid costly mistakes in market adjustments. This permits us to believe that more than ever this modeling approach can provide decision makers an extremely useful policy analysis tool.

In the present paper we have shown the flexibility of the approach which is able to compute a whole class of equilibria under different assumptions concerning the demand formation. We have also shown that imperfect market structure giving rise to Nash or Stackelberg equilibria can be captured through well designed mathematical programming models. Finally we have addressed the very important issue of modeling uncertainty. Recent hardware and software advances can put, at the finger tips of decision makers, user friendly decision support systems which handle large scale data bases corresponding to energy-environment markets. Considering the sums which are invested in these energy systems, one of the best investments decision makers involved in the design of sound energy-environment policies could do is to develop this type of methodology to assess the fundamental choices they have to make.

References

Baillard-Haurie, D., C. Berger, A. Haurie, R. Loulou and G. Savard, 1987, "What does \$15 versus \$23 Oil Mean for Long-Range Energy Choices in the Province of Québec?," *Canadian Public Policy*, Vol. 13, No. 1, pp. 56-61.

Bard, J.F. and Falk, J.E., 1982, "An Explicit Solution to the Multilevel Programming Problem," *Computers and Operations Research*, Vol.9, No.1, pp. 77-100.

Berger C., Dubois R., Haurie A., Lessard E., Loulou R. and Waaub J-P., 1992, "Canadian Markal: An Advanced Linear Programming System for Energy and Environmental Modelling," *INFOR*, vol. 30, no. 3, pp.222-239.

Berger C., Lessard E., Loulou R. and Waaub J-P., 1991, "Exploring Acid Gas Emission Reduction in the Province of Quebec via MARKAL-Quebec," *Energy Studies Review*, vol. 3, no. 2, pp.124-141.

Berger C., Loulou R., Soucy J.P. and Waaub J-P., 1991, "CO^2-Control in Quebec and Ontario," ETSAP/IIASA meeting , Laxenburg.

Berger, C., Dubois, R., Haurie, A. and Loulou, R., 1990a, "Modeling Electricity Trading in the Northeast," Proceedings of the 1990 Conference of the International Association of Energy Economics, Ottawa, October 1990.

Berger C., Fuller, C.D., Haurie, A., Loulou R., Luthra D. and Waaub J-P., 1990, "Modeling Energy Use in the Mineral Processing Industries of Ontario with MARKAL-Ontario," *Energy*, vol. 15, no. 9,pp.741-758.

Berger C., Haurie A., Loulou R., Lafrance G., Savard G. and Surprenant J-P., 1987, "MEDEQ-MARKAL: un couplage entre deux modéles technico-économiques du systéme énergétique du Québec," *RAIRO recherche opérationnelle*, vol. 21, pp. 21-50.

Bertsekas D.P., 1987, *Dynamic Programming: Deterministic and Sto-chastic Models*, Prentice Hall.

Bialas, W.F. and Karwan, M.H., 1982, "On Two-Level Optimization," *IEEE Transactions on Automatic Control*, vol.Ac-27, no.1, pp.211-214.

Birge, J.R. and Holmes, D.F, "Efficient Solution of Two Stage Stochastic Linear Programs Using Interior Point Methods," *Computational Optimization and Applications*, forthcoming.

Breton, A., Haurie, A. and Kalocsay, R., 1978, "Efficient Management of Interconnected Power Systems: A game theoretic Approach," *Automatica*, vol.14, pp. 443-452.

Dantzig, G.B., 1963, *Linear programming and Extensions*, Princeton University Press, Princeton, N.J.

Fishbone, L.G. and Abilock, H., 1981, "MARKAL, A Linear Programming Model for Energy Systems Analysis: Technical Description of the BHL Version," *International Journal of Energy Research,* vol. 5, pp.353-375.

Goffin, J.L., Haurie A., Vial, J.P. 1992{\rm a}, "Decomposition and Nondifferentiable Optimization with the Projective Algorithm," *Management science*, 38, pp. 284-302.

Goffin, J.L., Haurie A., Vial, J.P., Zhu, D.L. 1993a, "Using Central Prices in the Decomposition of Linear Programs," *European Journal of Operations*

Research, 64, no.3, pp.393-409.

Goffin J.L., Vial J.P., Bahn O., du Merle O.,1993, "A Cutting Plane Method from Analytic Centers for Stochastic Programming," Technical Report, Uni. Geneva.

Loulou, R., and J-P. Waaub, 1992, "CO^2 Control with Cooperation in Québec and Ontario: A MARKAL Perspective," *Energy Studies Review*, vol. 4, no.3.

Goldstein, G., 1991, "PC-MARKAL and the MARKAL Users Support System (MUSS), User's Guide," Brookhaven National Laboratory, Report BNL-46319.

Greenberg, H.J. and Murphy, F.H.,1985, "Computing Regulated Market Equilibria with Mathematical Programming," *Operations Research*, vol. 33, pp. 935-954.

Haurie, A., Loulou, R. and Savard, G., 1992, "A Two-Player Game Model of Power Cogeneration in New England," *IEEE Transactions on Automatic Control*, vol. 37, pp 1451-1456.

Haurie, A., Smeers Y. and Zaccour G., 1990, S-adapted equilibria, JOTA.

Hogan, W.W. and Weyant J.P., 1983, "Methods and Algorithms for Energy Model Composition: Optimization in a networkof process models," in: *Leved. Energy Models and Studies, North-Holland*, Amsterdam.

Loulou, R., G., Savard and D. Lavigne, 1993, Decomposition of Multi-Player Linear Programs, Annals of Dynamic Games, forthcoming in vol. 1.

Luenberger, D.G., 1973, *Introduction to Linear and Nonlinear Programming*, Addison Wesley, Reading, Mass.

Manne, A.S. and Richels, G., 1991, "International Trade in Carbon Emission Rights: A decomposition Procedure," American Economic Association Papers and Proceedings, vol. 81, no. 2.

Manne, A.S. and Richels, G., 1992, *Buying Greenhouse Insurance*, MIT Press, Cambridge, Mass.

Markowitz, H.M., 1959, Portfolio Selection. *Efficient Diversification of Investments*, Yale University Press, New Haven, Connecticut.

Murphy, F.H.,1987, "Equation Partitioning Techniques for Solving Partal Equilibrium Models," *European Journal of Operational Research*, vol. 32, pp.380-392.

Pellegrin, J.P., 1984, Un outil d'analyse de la demande énergitique à long terme: la méthode MEDEE et son application au cas du Québec, in L'implantation de MEDEE 3 au Québec: la méthodologie et les résultats, *Collection Études et Recherches*, Gouvernement du Québec, Ministère de l'Énergie et des ressources, Août 1984.

Rockafellar, R.T. and Wets, R.J.B., 1987, "Scenario and Policy Aggregation in Optimization under Uncertainty," IIASA Working Paper WP-87-119, Laxenburg, Austria.

Rosen, J.B., 1965, "Existence and uniqueness of equilibrium points for concave N-person games," *Econometrica,* 520-534.

Rubinstein, R.Y., 1986, *Monte-Carlo Optimization, Simulation and sensitivity of Queuing Networks*,Wiley, New York, NY.

Savard, G., Loulou, R., Lavigne, D., 1993, unpublished research.

Shapley, L.S., 1953, "A Value for *n*-Person Games, Annals of Mathematics Studies," vol. 8, no. 2, *Contributions to the Theory of Games*, vol. II, Edited by (H.W. Kuhn and A.W. Tucker},Princeton University Press, Princeton, N.J., pp. 307-317.

Wene, C.-O. and Ryden,B., 1988, A Comptrehensive Energy Model in theMunicipal Energy Planning Process, *European Journal of Operational Research*, vol. 33, no. 2, pp.212-222.

Wets, R.J.B., 1987, The aggregation Principle in Scenario Analysis and Stochastic Optimization, 1989 Mimeo.

Chapter 7
Relative Contribution of
the Enhanced Greenhouse Effect on the
Coastal Changes in Louisiana

Imma J. Curiel
Jerzy A. Filar
Radoslaw Zapert

Introduction

The *enhanced greenhouse effect* has been studied extensively during the past two decades. Although there is no conclusive proof that global warming is actually taking place, there is scientific consensus that human activities are causing global climatic changes. Currently, large scale simulation models provide the best insight into the anticipated global climatic changes. However, to estimate the impacts of the enhanced greenhouse effect on a particular region it is clearly necessary to combine global trends with the local trends in that region using an integrated technique rather than a large scale model.

In this paper we combine the outputs from IMAGE; the Dutch integrated greenhouse model (Rotmans, 1990) with local studies of the Louisiana coastline (Penland *et al.*, 1989; McBride *et al.*, 1991) in order to estimate the relative importance of the enhanced greenhouse effect on the Louisiana coastline.

The main conclusions of our study are:

- The contributions to Louisiana's coastal retreat changes from the enhanced greenhouse effect, while significant, are small comparing to the local geological and hydrological processes that are already altering Louisiana's coastline. Generally, the fractions of a total impact that can be contributed to the enhanced greenhouse effect lie between 2 and 31 percent.

- By combining local studies with an integrated global model we demonstrate that it is now possible to easily simulate the effect of world emission scenarios on a local scale. Indeed a user can now interactively enter his/her own global scenario and observe the simulated effects on Louisiana's coastline.

- Uncertainties in both the global and local effects models can severely affect the outcomes. Thus there is a need for a more detailed error analysis.

The IMAGE model has been designed and implemented at RIVM, the

Dutch National Institute of Public Health and Environmental Protection. It is accompanied by interactive software that runs on IBM compatible personal computers. As part of the present study a software package called SEAL was developed that interfaces with IMAGE and produces local impacts estimates for Louisiana's coastline.[1]

Background

Sea level has fluctuated throughout time. Sea level change at any location consists of a local component and a global component. Global sea level depends primarily on three factors: the total amount of water in the Earths oceans; the temperature of the water which determines its density; and the shape of the oceans' basins. The two first factors are influenced by global climate change while the last one is not. Compared to the first two factors, changes in the shape of the oceans' basins play a role only over a much longer period of time. Because of the recent concern about possible global warming caused by the enhanced greenhouse effect it is the first two of the above factors that we shall be concerned with.

Climatic changes and specifically an increase in the average temperature of the Earth are likely to influence the total amount of water in the oceans by affecting glaciers and small ice caps and the large ice masses of Greenland and Antarctica. Global warming will also influence sea level rise through thermal expansion of ocean water. Global sea level rise is a potential threat that should be taken seriously. A large part of the Earths population lives in close proximity to a coastline and sea level rise could endanger many lives if no precautions are taken. Physical consequences of sea level rise are: shoreline retreat and land loss due to inundation and erosion, increased salinity of the soil in coastal areas, increased salinity of aquifers in the coastal areas, and increase in the level of storm surges in the area that is inflicted by such a storm. All these factors will have socio-economic as well as environmental impacts.

Several studies have been conducted to determine the scope of the above mentioned physical consequences for certain areas in the U.S. For example a case study by Kana, *et al.*, 1984) considered Charleston, South Carolina. A study by Leatherman, (1984) was devoted to the Galveston Bay, Texas. Gibbs, (1984) gives an economic analysis of the physical effects of sea level rise for these two

---

[1] Both models, SEAL and IMAGE 1.0 have been integrated into a single software package WIM available from the authors upon request. SEAL can be obtained from the authors, upon request. However, SEAL requires 1991 IMAGE version 1.0 to run.

areas. He also gives an analysis of the benefits of anticipating the rise. For the Delaware estuary a case study was performed to estimate the effect of increased salinity due to sea level rise (Hull & Titus, 1986). The EPA report: 'Greenhouse effect, sea level rise and coastal wetlands' edited by Titus, (1988) documents the effect of sea level rise on wetlands in the U.S. Since this paper is concerned with impacts on coastal regions of Louisiana it is worth noting that studies that specifically focus on the impacts of enhanced greenhouse effect on that region are not easily found. However, we made extensive use of a number of studies dealing with local trends of coastal erosion in Louisiana (Britsch *et al.*, 1990; Costanza *et al.*, 1983; Dunbar *et al.*, 1990 & 1992; McBride *et al.*, 1991; and Penland *et al.*, 1989).

The Enhanced Greenhouse Effect and the Dutch IMAGE Model
The Greenhouse Effect and the Sea Level Rise

The physical phenomenon of the trapping of the surface infrared radiation by the so called greenhouse gases, such as CO_2, CH_4, CO, N_2O, O_3, $CFCs$ and H_2O[2] is called the *greenhouse effect*. The incoming solar shortwave radiation is absorbed by the Earths surface and re-emitted as longwave radiation. Some fraction of this radiation is then trapped by the above mentioned greenhouse gases before being emitted back into space. This process is responsible for increasing the average surface temperature of the Earth from approximately -18 $^\circ C$[3] to approximately 15 $^\circ C$ thereby allowing life on Earth, as we know it, to flourish. With the exception, perhaps, of water vapor (H_2O) the atmospheric concentrations of other greenhouse gases have been increasing as a direct consequence of human activities. This has led to worldwide concern that the increasing concentrations of these gases will lead to the increasing absorption rates of the longwave radiation and hence will *enhance* the greenhouse effect to the point that will affect climate on a global scale, with *global warming* being the most likely result.

Since the beginning of the industrial revolution the concentrations of the greenhouse gases in the atmosphere have increased considerably, mostly due to combustion of fossil fuels. Measurements show an increase of CO_2 concentrations

---

[2] CO_2 - carbon dioxide, CH_4 - methane, CO - carbon monoxide, N_2O - nitroux oxide, O_3 - ozone, $CFCs$ - chlorofuorocarbons, and H_2O - water.

[3] $^\circ C$ - degree Celsius.

from 315 *ppmv*[4] in 1958 to *339 ppmv* in 1980 (Keeling, 1982). The expectation is that these increased concentrations will lead to an enhancement of the greenhouse effect and a global warming of the Earth. Opinions differ about the extent of this warming. The difficulties arise mainly from the uncertainty in the effects of climatic feedbacks. It is expected that global warming of the Earth would induce a sea level rise by causing thermal expansion of ocean water, melting of mountain glaciers and influencing the ice cover of Greenland and Antarctica.

Several studies have dealt with these issues. Revelle, (1983) gives an estimate of 70 *cm* +/- 17 *cm*[5] of the total sea level rise for the year 2085, consisting of 12 *cm* rise due to melting of the Greenland ice cap, 12 *cm* rise due to the melting of mountain glaciers, 30 *cm* rise due to thermal expansion, and 16 *cm* rise due to other causes. The National Academy of Sciences Polar Research Board report: 'Glaciers, ice sheets, and sea level' by Meier, *et al.*, 1985 estimates that alpine and Greenland glaciers will each contribute 10 *cm* to 30 *cm* to the sea level rise by the year 2100. The Antarctic contribution is estimated to be anywhere from a 10 *cm* drop to a 100 *cm* rise. Hoffman, *et al.*, 1986) give the following estimates for the year 2100: contribution due to alpine glaciers 12 *cm* to 37 *cm* rise, contribution due to the Greenland ice cap melting 6 *cm* to 27 *cm* rise, contribution due to thermal expansion 28 *cm* to 83 *cm* rise, and contribution due to Antarctica ice cap melting 12 *cm* to 220 *cm* rise, leading to a total of 57 *cm* to 368 *cm* rise. Thomas, (1986) gives the following estimates of the sea level rise: alpine glaciers melting *cm* to 35 *cm*, Greenland ice cap melting 9 *cm* to 45 *cm*, thermal expansion 28 *cm* to 70 *cm*, Antarctica ice cap melting 13 *cm* to 80 *cm*, for a total of 64 *cm* to 230 *cm* rise.

IMAGE - Integrated Greenhouse Effect Model

IMAGE; an Integrated Model to Assess the Greenhouse Effect is computer simulation model based on scientific principles, developed to estimate historical and future emissions of greenhouse gases and their effect on global temperature and sea level rise (Rotmans, 1990). IMAGE was developed at the National Institute of Public Health and Environmental Protection in the Netherlands (RIVM) by Rotmans and his group. The greenhouse problem is modeled as a dynamical system evolving in time with simulation period from 1900

---

[4]*ppmv* - parts per million per volume.

[5]*cm* - centimeter, 1.0 *cm* = 0.01 *m* (meter).

to 2100. Mathematically the model is represented by a system of first order ordinary differential equations, and algebraic equations.

The system has a modular structure. At the highest aggregation level it consists of the following modules: greenhouse gases emission module, greenhouse gases concentration module, climate change module, sea level rise module, and socio-economic impact module for the Netherlands. Each module consists in itself of submodules.

To model emissions IMAGE implements four environmental scenarios, each one making consistent assumptions about the world emissions of greenhouse gases and related land use activities. These scenarios are meant to illustrate the impact of different strategies with respect to economic development on the greenhouse effect. Scenario A or *Unrestricted Trends* or *Business as Usual*, assumes a continuation of economic development without any environmental considerations. Scenario B or *Reduced Trends*, considers the situation where implemented measures are influenced by other environmental problems than the greenhouse effect, e.g., acid rain and the ozone hole. Scenario C or *Changed Trends*, assumes that stricter environmental control will be enforced, at least partly influenced by concern about the greenhouse effect. Finally, scenario D or *Forced Trends*, models a situation where maximum efforts are being made towards global sustainable development. Importantly, IMAGE also has the interactive capability that allows a user to construct his/her own world emissions scenario. It is the atmospheric concentration of the greenhouse gases that drives the greenhouse effect.

To model this IMAGE considers, for each gas separately, all the processes involved in removing it from the atmosphere. In the case of CO_2 for example this requires a link of emissions module with an ocean module, a terrestrial biosphere module and a deforestation module. The concentrations of each gas are used as inputs for the climate module. The sea level rise module uses the temperature rise calculated in the climate module to estimate the four components of sea level rise: thermal expansion, alpine glaciers melting, Greenland and Antarctica ice caps melting/expanding. Finally, the socio-economic impact module for the Netherlands uses the result of the sea level rise module to estimate costs of adjusting the coastal defense and costs of changes in water management in the Netherlands.

Methodology and the Results

Louisiana, located in the delta of the Mississippi River and the Gulf of

Mexico, has a very large coastal zone and extremely long, 624 km^6, Gulf coastline. This coastal zone, situated at a very low altitude, is vulnerable to the tropical storms, sea currents, salt intrusion, and other hydrological phenomena. These processes may have a magnified effect if the sea level rise in the region is accelerated by the greenhouse effect, with particularly severe impact in the Louisiana's unique deltaic - estuarine ecosystem in the delta of the Mississippi River. Therefore, the sea level rise is perceived as one of the major causes of the degradation of the Louisiana coastal zone. It is virtually impossible to analyze all the effects of the accelerated sea level rise in that area, because of the high complexity of the ecosystems and the lack of accurate data describing coastal erosion. Since such a detailed analysis was not realistic, we decided to select a number of quantities representing a variety of possible consequences of the sea level rise in different geographical locations. This approach will give us a more general indication of the magnitude and extent of the accelerated sea level rise impact in the discussed region.

Description of the Area and the Variables

We focused our attention on the Eastern Terrebonne Parish because the data for that area were the most comprehensive. There are three groups of variables present in our analysis. The first group is associated with the erosion of the barrier islands, the second group with the land loss on the Louisiana coastal plain, and the last group with salt intrusion in the marsh areas. We also model a variable representing sea level rise in the region. This quantity plays a crucial role in the analysis since all the other variables are calculated on its basis. The sea level rise is measured at the Houma Tide gage station lying on the Inter-coastal waterway and operated by the US Corps of Engineers. We assume that sea level rise measured at this location is representative of the entire Eastern Terrebonne Parish. Historical data for the period 1942 - 1985 comes from the Louisiana geological report on the relative sea level rise in Louisiana (Penland *et al.*, 1989). This report identifies seven factors of the sea level rise:

- Global sea level rise
- Geosyncline downwarping
- Compaction of Tertiary and Pleistocene deposits
- Compaction of Holocene deposits

---

^6km - kilometer, 1.0 km = 1000.0 m (meters).

- Consolidation
- Tectonic activity
- Subsurface fluid withdrawal.

The first factor reflects a sea level rise on the global scale, independent of the local geophysical processes and associated with the greenhouse effect factors like thermal expansion of the oceans and ice caps or glaciers melting. The remaining six components correspond to the processes having local character and thus independent of the global warming factor.

The first region of interest to us are the systems of barrier islands. There are four such complexes along the Mississippi River delta plain: Isles Dernieres, Bayou Lafourche, Plaquemines, and Chandeleur Islands. They have been formed in reworking of the abandoned Mississippi River deltas. These islands play an important role in responding to the impact of tropical and extratropical storms. The total length of the barrier islands coastline is approximately 240 *km*. In our analysis we consider only two of the four systems: Isles Dernieres and Bayou Lafourche.

Isles Dernieres, a continuous deltaic headland a hundred years ago, at present has become fragmented into five islands: East, Raccoon, Trinity, Whiskey, and Wine, of the combined shoreline of 35 *km*. As a consequence of the sea level rise and storm activity, the islands diminish quickly as a result of shoreline erosion. Both the gulf side and the bay side shore lines converge and ultimately will cause the disappearance of the islands. This process is more extensive on the gulf side because of the storm activity. We consider five impact variables associated with the length of each island's gulf side shoreline retreat compared to the 1990 status. The sixth variable represents the total area change of the Isles Dernieres combining the land loss of the five islands. It is worth mentioning that during the last hundred years Isles Dernieres has suffered a 78% land loss. Bayou Lafourche barrier system with 65 *km* long shoreline, consists of two parts: Timbalier Islands and Caminada - Moreau Headland and Grand Isle.

We will concentrate on the first part, that is, Timbalier Islands, constituted of the East Timbalier Island and Timbalier Island. Similarly to the previous case we distinguish two variables describing the islands gulf side shoreline retreat and the third variable indicating their area change. The data for the barrier islands have been obtained from the paper of McBride, *et al.*, (1991) devoted to the mapping of changes of the Louisiana barrier islands.

Louisiana coastal plain is the second region of our interest. The data for this part comes from the reports of Britsch and Kemp, (1990) and Dunbar, (1992) describing the land loss in the 62 USGS 15 minutes quadrangle maps of the Louisiana coastal plain. We selected a representative sample of four areas in that region: Dulac, Lake Felicity, Terrebonne Bay, and Timbalier Bay and associated with each area a variable representing its respective land loss.[7]

The third and the last group of variables describes the effects of salt intrusion and a direct sea action on the marsh areas in the Eastern Terrebonne Parish. We distinguish three categories of marshes: 1) fresh marsh - the natural, fresh water marsh, not affected by salt intrusion, 2) saline marsh - degraded by salt intrusion, 3) water area - representing further degradation of marshes, the area completely covered by the salt water. With the marsh area of each type we associate a variable measuring the change compared to the year 1990.

Mathematical Model

We will refer to the variables described in the above section as the impact variables except for the sea level rise at Houma variable which we will simply call sea level rise. Our model is based on the following assumptions:

1. We relate all the variables including sea level rise to their state in 1990 which means that they measure the change compared to 1990 and thus have values of 0 in 1990.

2. All the variables specified above are assumed to have a component proportional to the sea level rise in the region and the remaining component that is linear in time.

3. The proportionality coefficients from the assumption **2**, calculated from historical data, remain unchanged over the period of time 1990 - 2100.

4. The local component of the sea level rise is linear in time between 1900 and 2100.

5. We assume that the sea level rise in the region is accurately represented by the sea level rise measured at the Houma tide gage station.

The error estimates are taken from the cited literature. The most comprehensive error analysis is provided by McBride, *et al.*, (1991) report on barrier Islandsand Penland, *et al.*, (1989) report on land subsidence and sea level rise in Louisiana. Other sources give little, if any, information about the error estimates.

In the view of the above assumptions the most important variable in the

---

[7]Note: Timbalier Islands and Timbalier Bay are two different geographical regions.

analysis is the sea level rise. We denote that variable by S(t) for the time t satisfying $1990 = t_0 < t < 2100$. As mentioned earlier, S(t) has two components: local $S_l(t)$ and global $S_g(t)$. From the assumption **1** we have that:

$$S(t_0) = S_1(t_0) = S_g(t_0) = 0. \tag{1}$$

From the assumptions **4** and **5** we have:

$$S(t) = S_1(t) + S_g(t) = L_s(t_1 - t_0) + S_g(t), \tag{2}$$

where L_s is the annual local trend.

The values of $S_g(t)$ are obtained from the IMAGE model simulation and $S_l(t)$ has to be estimated. In order to estimate L_s and hence $S_l(t)$ we have to combine S(t) estimates and the $S_g(t)$ from IMAGE. Penland *et al.*, (1989) gives the estimated 1.31 +/- 0.15 *cm/yr*[8] of the sea level rise over the period 1942 - 1985. The corresponding IMAGE estimate of the global trend value is 0.15 *cm/yr*. Thus the annual local trend at Houma is $L_s = 1.16$ +/- 0.15 *cm/yr* and:

$$S_1(t) = 1.16(t_1 - t_0). \tag{3}$$

We also define, for $t > t_0$, a quantity:

$$R_s(t) = \frac{S_g(t)}{S(t)}, \tag{4}$$

as a *relative greenhouse effect contribution* to the sea level rise at Houma. This quantity will measure the fraction of the sea level rise caused by the greenhouse effect related processes. From the assumptions **2** and **3** the generic model for a given impact variable Y(t) is:

$$Y(t) = A_y S(t) + B_y(t - t_0), \tag{5}$$

where S(t) is the sea level rise, A_y is the proportionality factor between Y(t) and

---

[8] *cm/yr* - centimeters per year.

$S(t)$, and $B_y(t-t_0)$ is the impact variable component independent of $Y(t)$. To be consistent, we define $Y_g(t)$ as a global component of $Y(t)$ and $Y(t)$ the local component of $Y(t)$ as follows:

$$\begin{aligned} Y(t) &= A_y(S_1(t) + S_g(t)) + B_y(t-t_0) \\ &= (A_y L_s + B_y)(t-t_0) + A_y S_g(t) \\ &= Y_1(t) + Y_g(t), \end{aligned} \tag{6}$$

and the relative greenhouse effect contribution will be defined as:

$$R_y(t) = \frac{Y_g(t)}{Y(t)}, \tag{7}$$

Because of a potential presence of the nonzero B_y coefficient and the nature of the data, it is convenient to consider the annual increments of the variables rather then the variables. Thus we define:

$$\Delta Y(t) = Y(t+1) - Y(t), \tag{8}$$

and

$$\Delta S(t) = S(t+1) - S(t), \tag{9}$$

and

$$\Delta Y(t) = A_y \Delta S(t) + B_y, \tag{10}$$

where the coefficients A_y and B_y can be identified from a linear regression model applied to the data

$$(\Delta S_j, \Delta Y_j) \; for \; j = 1, \ldots, k, \tag{11}$$

where:

$$\Delta S_j = \Delta S(t_j), \qquad \Delta Y_j = \Delta Y(t_j), \tag{12}$$

and,

$$t_0 < t_1 < \ldots < t_k. \tag{13}$$

In the case of barrier islands we have to account for one more factor. The islands are likely to disappear under the water during the next century. There are estimates t_y of when this will happen assuming a linear continuation of the present trends and thus not accounting for the progressive character of the global sea level rise. Since it is meaningless to consider the shoreline retreat after the island disappears under the water we have to establish the cut off values C_y such that:

$$Y(t) = \min [C_t, Y(t)], \tag{14}$$

where C_y can be calculated from the estimated disappearance time t_y of the given island as follows:

$$C_y = Y(t_y) - Y_g(t_y) = (A_y L_s + B_y)(t_y - t_0). \tag{15}$$

For barrier islands we define a quantity T_y representing a time delay defined as a difference between the time when the island disappears if the erosion process is accelerated by the greenhouse effect sea level rise and t_y, that is:

$$T_y = \min[t \,|\, Y(t) > C_y] - t_y. \tag{16}$$

Note that T_y depends on $Y_g(t)$ and hence on $S_g(t)$ and thus on the environmental policy implemented in the next century. The same conclusion applies to any of the impact variables $Y(t)$. Therefore, by changing such emission policy we can observe the changes in the $Y(t)$, $R_y(t)$ and T_y values. From the above it follows that a given impact variable $Y(t)$ may be characterized by the three coefficients: A_y, B_y, C_y in the case of the barrier islands, and by A_y and B_y in all other cases.

Below we give a list of corresponding coefficients for all of the impact variables. Note that (*) indicates that there is no cut off value for the variable, *sqm* denotes square miles, *ha* hectares, % percent of the 1990 value, Error denotes the error estimate derived from the data cited in the McBride and Penland reports, (?) indicates the lack of error estimates.

Table 7-1
Descriptions of model's variables

Variable	Description	A_y	B_y	C_y	Error
Y_1	East Island shoreline retreat	4.60 *m/cm*	0.00 *m/yr*	160.1 *m*	3.42 *m/cm*
Y_2	Raccoon Island shoreline retreat	9.20 *m/cm*	0.00 *m/yr*	106.7 *m*	2.43 *m/cm*
Y_3	Trinity Island shoreline retreat	9.40 *m/cm*	0.00 *m/yr*	381.1 *m*	1.76 *m/cm*
Y_4	Whiskey Island shoreline retreat	15.8 *m/cm*	0.00 *m/yr*	641.7 *m*	3.41 *m/cm*
Y_5	Wine Island shoreline retreat	17.5 *m/cm*	0.00 *m/yr*	101.5 *m*	1.85 *m/cm*
Y_6	East Timbalier Island shoreline retreat	11.3 *m/cm*	0.00 *m/yr*	208.8 *m*	4.40 *m/cm*
Y_7	Timbalier Island shoreline retreat	3.60 *m/cm*	0.00 *m/yr*	655.4 *m*	4.48 *m/cm*
Y_8	Isles Dernieres area change	10.2 *ha/cm*	27.5 *m/yr*	*	?
Y_9	Timbalier Islands area change	33.5 *ha/cm*	6.50 *m/yr*	*	?
Y_{10}	Dulac area change	0.60 *sqm/cm*	0.33 *m/yr*	*	?
Y_{11}	Lake Felicity area change	0.61 *sqm/cm*	0.25 *m/yr*	*	?
Y_{12}	Terrebonne Bay area change	0.11 *sqm/cm*	0.17 *m/yr*	*	?
Y_{13}	Timbalier Bay area change	0.06 *sqm/cm*	0.21 *m/yr*	*	?
Y_{14}	Fresh Marsh area decrease	0.30 *%/cm*	0.00 *%/yr*	*	?
Y_{15}	Non - Fresh Marsh area decrease	0.10 *%/cm*	0.00 *%/yr*	*	?
Y_{16}	Water Area increase	0.20 *%/cm*	0.00 *%/yr*	*	?

Results

In order to asses the enhanced greenhouse effect's contribution to the impact variables we decided to implement two of the four standard scenarios provided by IMAGE. They represent certain models of the development of the human population in the next century. The two selected scenarios describe extreme approaches to the environment. Scenario A or *Business as Usual* scenario is the most environmentally insensitive with unlimited fossil fuel usage and thus exponentially growing greenhouse gases emissions. Scenario D, to the contrary, assumes enforcement of the strict environmental policies resulting in

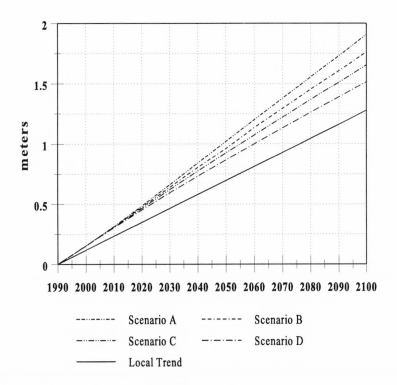

Figure 7-1
Sea level rise at Houma tide gage station. Local trend
S_l **and four standard scenarios** S^A, S^B, S^C, **and** S^D, **see table 7-2.**

stabilization of the greenhouse gases emissions at a very low level. Any other practically feasible scenario would have the emissions contained between these two extreme scenarios. Figure 7-1 presents the sea level rise according to the four standard scenarios and local trend at Houma.

Thus we may conclude that the possible impact of the enhanced greenhouse effect for any emission policy has to be contained in the range defined by the outcomes of scenarios A and D. To illustrate this we implement our own scenarios, denoted K and L, which assume a stabilization of emissions starting in 2025 (L) and 2000 (K), respectively. They both coincide with scenario A before the leveling off takes place. It could be argued that scenarios K and L approximate the situations when enforceable international agreements on greenhouse gas emissions are reached and enforced in the years 2000 and 2025, respectively. Figures 7-2, and 7-3 present examples of the behavior of typical impact variables. Table 7-2 in the Appendix contains the numerical results of the simulations for the above mentioned scenarios.

The variable numbers and units correspond to the notation used in table 7-1. Now we summarize the results of simulating the four scenarios A, K, L, and D on the sea level rise and the local impact variables listed in the table 7-1. Note that in the table 7-2 the S corresponds to the sea level rise at Houma, Y_i corresponds to the i-th impact variable from table 7-1. and superscripts indicate under which scenario a given variable is calculated. All the figures are expressed in units from table 7-1. For instance, 102.8 in row 28 and column 4 means that the gulf side shore line retreat of the East Timbalier Island under scenario D, by the year 2010 is estimated to be 102.8 m, that is $Y_6^D(2010) = 102.8$ m.

From table 7-2 we can make the following observations:

- The sea level rise in the Eastern Terrebonne Parish is affected by the greenhouse effect in the amount of only 11.1% to 30.6% due to a very strong local trend, which we attribute largely to the land subsidence processes. Any emission policy implemented in the next century could account for only up to 40.4 cm difference in the sea level rise while the local trend (scenario - independent) is 127.6 cm by the year 2100. The same figure for 2050 shows only 16.5 cm difference between A and D versus 70.0 cm of the local trend. Similar conclusions apply to the other impact variables; in all cases the enhanced greenhouse effect would contribute even less to the total effect than in the case of sea level rise variable.

- The time delay of disappearance of the barrier islands varies from 0 to 13 years and the maximal difference between scenarios A and D occurs for the East Timbalier Island and is equal to 5 years. The relative greenhouse effect contribution varies from 18.0% to 28.0% in this process in the year 2100. The area loss of the barrier islands due to the enhanced greenhouse effect is in the range of 3.6% to 27.6% of the total area loss in the year 2100.

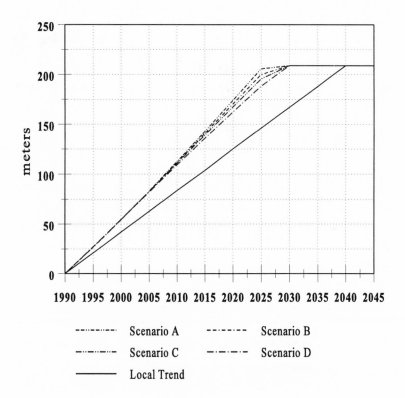

Figure 7-2
Timbalier Island shore line retreat (Y_7). Four standard scenarios and the corresponding local trend.

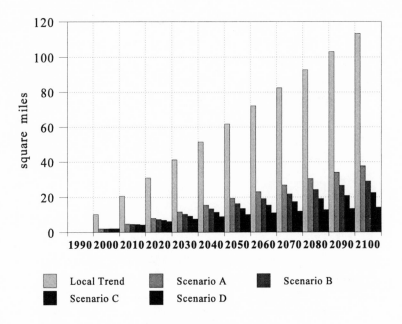

Figure 7-3
Dulac area change (Y_{10}). Greenhouse effect
contributions for four standard scenarios and the
corresponding local trend.

- The Louisiana coastal plain land loss due to the enhanced greenhouse effect is in the range of 4.9% to 24.6% of the total area lost by the year 2100. The figures for habitat change are similar to those for the sea level rise since these variables are linear functions of S(t). The general conclusions from the above observations are as follows: The gap between scenario A and D impact is widening in time, while the effects of the enhanced greenhouse effect in the first case become more significant the role of this phenomenon in the second case increases for about 20 - 30 years and then decreases when the emission restrictions in scenario D start to have an impact.

- A comparison between scenarios L and K is interesting. They follow scenario A to 2025 and 2000 respectively and then instantaneously stabilize all the human greenhouse gas emissions. The result of such an experiment is that at the year 2050, that is 25 and respectively 50 years after the emission stabilization the difference between impact variables is minimal. For example sea level rise is only 6.5 *cm* lower in 2050 according to the scenario K than in the scenario L. The differences between these scenarios becomes more significant in 2100. This exhibits a large inertia of the global climate system in response to the greenhouse gas emission changes.

Our experiment shows that results of enforcing radical environmental policies are apparent only a few decades later; which means at least one human generation later. Local trends in the processes modeled by impact variables are very strong in Louisiana, so strong that the additional effect of the global sea level rise is moderate and in some cases completely insignificant. On the other hand, the accuracy of measurements of local trends is not very precise and this causes a major source of uncertainty in model predictions. It can be seen from the table 7-1 that the error estimates are very large and some of them account for 10% to 55% of the variable value.

By the same argument error involved in the global sea level rise prediction according to IMAGE will have only minor effect on the accuracy of the impact variables. Another important reason to study the local trends is to model more realistically the dependence of impact variables on the global and local sea level rise components. We use simple linear relationship describing this process and it may not be the most realistic approach to the problem. However, linear regression model was virtually the only choice, given the available data.

SEAL a computer implementation of the model

The RIVM integrated model of the enhanced greenhouse effect provides a convenient platform for building local impact modules interfacing with IMAGE. Its user friendly design enabled us to implement and link with IMAGE our accelerated sea level rise impact model for Louisiana, called SEAL. SEAL provides an attractive method for practical simulation and analysis of the global environmental emission scenarios, in terms of their impact on the Louisiana coastal zone. The main purpose of the SEAL software is to calculate the impact variables according to the model presented above. Our intention was to offer the policy makers and other people interested in the problem a tool that allows them to asses the consequences of the greenhouse effect on a small, local, scale. Another important reason for creating SEAL was to further demonstrate the usefulness of the integrated approach to the greenhouse problem.

SEAL has been designed as an additional IMAGE module, which uses IMAGE's predictions of the future global sea level rise. Using SEAL consists of two stages: 1) Running IMAGE and thus implementing certain environmental strategy, and 2) Calling SEAL which extracts the sea level data and then calculates the impact variables. SEAL computes all the quantities defined above. It has capability of displaying the results in various ways using sophisticated graphical interface that can emphasize different aspects of the problem. SEAL is easy to use but, of course, it requires the knowledge of using IMAGE since it cannot function without the IMAGE data. Its big advantage is portability; SEAL can be used on virtually any IBM PC compatible computer able to run IMAGE. It is also easily expandable, as the new impact variables are specified one can very easily incorporate them into the program. The current version of SEAL, release 1.0, November 1992, does not provide error estimation or a variability analysis.[9]

---

[9]SEAL model integrated with IMAGE 1.0 in the WIM software package includes the above mentioned features. It is available from the authors, upon request. We hope to add these features in the subsequent This will enhance SEAL's capability and will make this model more reliable. Copies of the SEAL software with documentation are available upon request from the authors. IMAGE software may be obtained from RIVM.

Appendix

Table 7-2

Numerical results of simulations of scenarios A, L, K, and D.

Time	2000		2010		2020		2050		2100	
Var.	Value	Ry%	Value	Ry%	Value	Ry%	Value	Ry%	Value	Ry%
S^A	14.47	19.8	30.08	22.9	46.64	25.4	98.53	29.4	183.9	30.6
S^L	14.47	19.8	30.08	22.9	46.64	25.4	96.90	28.2	166.1	23.2
S^K	14.47	19.8	29.99	22.6	45.89	24.1	90.54	23.1	152.4	16.3
S^D	14.26	18.7	28.56	18.8	42.49	18.1	81.99	15.1	143.5	11.1
Y_1^A	66.55	19.8	138.4	22.9	160.1	26.7	160.1	26.7	160.1	26.7
Y_1^L	66.55	19.8	138.4	22.9	160.1	26.7	160.1	26.7	160.1	26.7
Y_1^K	66.55	19.8	138.4	22.6	160.1	26.7	160.1	26.7	160.1	26.7
Y_1^D	65.62	18.7	131.4	18.8	160.1	20.0	160.1	20.0	160.1	20.0
Y_2^A	106.7	20.0	106.7	20.0	106.7	20.0	106.7	20.0	106.7	20.0
Y_2^L	106.7	20.0	106.7	20.0	106.7	20.0	106.7	20.0	106.7	20.0
Y_2^K	106.7	20.0	106.7	20.0	106.7	20.0	1067	20.0	106.7	20.0
Y_2^D	106.7	20.0	106.7	20.0	106.7	20.0	1067	20.0	106.7	20.0
Y_3^A	136.0	19.8	282.7	22.9	381.6	25.7	381.6	25.7	381.6	25.7
Y_3^L	136.0	19.8	282.7	22.9	381.6	25.7	381.6	25.7	381.6	25.7
Y_3^K	136.0	19.8	280.9	22.6	381.6	25.7	381.6	25.7	381.6	25.7
Y_3^D	134.1	18.7	268.4	18.8	381.6	20.0	381.6	20.0	381.6	20.0
Y_4^A	228.6	19.8	475.3	22.9	641.5	25.7	641.5	25.7	641.5	25.7
Y_4^L	228.6	19.8	475.3	22.9	641.5	25.7	641.5	25.7	641.5	25.7
Y_4^K	228.6	19.8	473.9	22.6	641.5	25.7	641.5	25.7	641.5	25.7
Y_4^D	225.4	18.7	451.2	18.8	641.5	20.0	641.5	20.0	641.5	20.0
Y_5^A	101.5	20.0	101.5	20.0	101.5	20.0	101.5	20.0	101.5	20.0
Y_5^L	101.5	20.0	101.5	20.0	101.5	20.0	101.5	20.0	101.5	20.0
Y_5^K	101.5	20.0	101.5	20.0	101.5	20.0	101.5	20.0	101.5	20.0

Table 7-2 (Cont.)

Time	2000		2010		2020		2050		2100	
Var.	Value	Ry%	Value	Ry%	Value	Ry%	Value	Ry%	Value	Ry%
Y_5^D	101.5	20.0	101.5	20.0	101.5	20.0	101.5	20.0	101.5	20.0
Y_6^A	52.08	19.8	108.3	22.9	167.9	25.4	208.8	28.0	208.8	28.0
Y_6^L	52.08	19.8	108.3	22.9	167.9	25.4	208.8	28.0	208.8	28.0
Y_6^K	52.08	19.8	108.0	22.6	165.1	24.1	208.8	28.0	208.8	28.0
Y_6^D	51.35	18.7	102.8	18.8	153.0	18.1	208.8	18.0	208.8	18.0
Y_7^A	163.5	19.8	339.9	22.9	527.1	25.4	655.4	28.0	655.4	28.0
Y_7^L	163.5	19.8	339.9	22.9	527.1	25.4	655.4	28.0	655.4	28.0
Y_7^K	163.5	19.8	338.9	22.6	518.4	24.1	655.4	28.0	655.4	28.0
Y_7^D	161.2	18.6	322.7	18.8	480.2	18.1	655.4	18.0	655.4	18.0
Y_8^A	422.6	6.92	856.8	8.18	1301	9.28	2655	11.1	4901	11.7
Y_8^L	422.6	6.92	856.8	8.18	1301	9.28	2638	10.5	4720	8.32
Y_8^K	422.6	6.92	855.9	8.09	1293	8.73	2574	8.30	4580	5.52
Y_8^D	420.5	6.46	841.3	6.49	1258	6.23	2486	5.08	4489	3.62
Y_9^A	578.6	17.6	1198	20.4	1851	22.7	3888	26.4	7243	27.6
Y_9^L	578.6	17.6	1198	20.4	1851	22.7	3781	25.3	6613	20.7
Y_9^K	578.6	17.6	1195	20.2	1824	21.6	3604	20.6	6126	14.4
Y_{10}^D	571.4	16.6	1144	16.6	1703	16.0	3301	13.3	5810	9.74
Y_{10}^A	12.02	14.3	24.72	16.6	37.99	18.6	79.10	21.8	147.0	22.9
Y_{10}^L	12.02	14.3	24.72	16.6	37.99	18.6	78.13	20.9	136.4	16.9
Y_{10}^K	12.02	14.3	24.66	16.4	37.30	17.6	74.33	16.8	128.2	11.6
Y_{10}^D	11.09	13.4	23.81	13.4	35.51	12.9	69.23	10.7	122.9	7.74
Y_{11}^A	11.30	15.4	23.29	18.0	35.86	20.1	74.91	23.5	139.3	24.6
Y_{11}^L	11.30	15.4	23.29	18.0	35.86	20.1	73.91	22.5	128.5	18.2
Y_{11}^K	11.30	15.4	23.23	17.8	35.39	18.2	70.05	12.7	120.2	12.6
Y_{11}^D	11.17	14.5	22.36	14.6	33.34	14.0	64.85	11.6	114.8	8.44

Table 7-2 (Cont.)

Time	2000		2010		2020		2050		2100	
Var.	Value	Ry%	Value	Ry%	Value	Ry%	Value	Ry%	Value	Ry%
Y_{12}^A	3.219	9.36	6.558	11.0	9.998	12.4	20.55	14.8	38.01	15.6
Y_{12}^L	3.219	9.36	6.558	10.7	9.998	12.2	20.37	14.1	36.14	11.2
Y_{12}^K	3.219	9.36	6.549	10.9	9.917	11.7	19.71	11.2	34.70	7.50
Y_{12}^D	3.198	8.75	6.398	87.9	9.562	8.45	18.81	6.92	33.77	4.95
Y_{13}^A	2.900	5.47	5.863	6.49	8.879	7.38	18.05	8.86	33.27	9.36
Y_{13}^L	2.900	5.47	5.863	6.49	8.879	7.38	17.96	8.41	32.29	6.60
Y_{13}^K	2.900	5.47	5.859	6.41	8.837	6.93	17.61	6.58	31.53	4.35
Y_{13}^D	2.889	5.10	5.779	5.13	8.650	4.92	17.13	4.00	31.04	2.84
Y_{14}^A	4.340	19.9	9.024	22.9	13.99	25.4	29.41	29.4	55.03	30.6
Y_{14}^L	4.340	19.9	9.024	22.9	13.99	25.4	29.07	28.2	49.84	23.2
Y_{14}^K	4.340	19.9	8.997	22.6	13.76	241	27.16	23.1	45.73	16.3
Y_{14}^D	4.279	18.7	8.567	18.8	12.75	181	24.60	15.1	43.06	11.1
Y_{15}^A	1.447	19.9	3.008	22.9	4.664	25.4	9.805	29.4	18.34	30.6
Y_{15}^L	1.447	19.9	3.008	22.9	4.664	25.4	9.690	28.2	16.61	23.2
Y_{15}^K	1.447	19.9	2.999	22.6	4.587	24.1	9.054	23.1	15.24	16.3
Y_{15}^D	1.426	18.7	2.856	18.8	4.249	18.1	8.199	15.1	14.35	11.1
Y_{16}^A	2.894	19.9	5.977	22.9	9.329	25.4	19.61	29.4	36.69	30.6
Y_{16}^L	2.894	19.9	5.977	22.9	9.329	25.4	19.38	28.2	33.23	23.2
Y_{16}^K	2.894	19.9	5.998	22.6	9.175	24.1	18.11	23.1	30.48	16.3
Y_{16}^D	2.853	18.7	5.711	18.8	8.498	18.1	16.40	15.1	28.71	11.1

References

Barnett, T.P. (1983), Global sea level: estimating and explaining apparent changes. In: Magoon, O.T. (ed.), *Coastal Zone,* American Society of Civil Engineers, New York, 83: 2777-2795.

Barth, M.C. & Titus J.G. (eds.), (1984), *Greenhouse Effect and Sea Level Rise: A Challenge for this Generation.* Van Nostrand Reinhold Company Inc., New York.

Britsch, L.D. & Kemp, E.B. (1990), Land loss rates: Mississippi River deltaic plain. Technical Report G1-90-2, USACE District New Orleans.

Bruun, P. (1962), Sea level rise as a cause of shore erosion. *Journal of the Waterways and Harbors Division,* 88: 117-130.

Costanza, R., Neill, C., Leibowitz, S.G., Fruci, I.R., Bahr, L.M., Jr., & Day J.W., Jr. (1983), Ecological models of the Mississippi deltaic plain region: data collection and presentation. Technical Report FWS/OBS-82/68, U.S. Fish and Wildlife Service, Division of Biological Service, Washington D.C.

Dunbar, J.B., Britsch, L.D., & Kemp, E.B., 3rd (1990), Land loss rates: Louisiana Chenier plain. Technical Report GL- 90-2, USACE District, New Orleans.

Dunbar, J.B., Britsch, L.D., & Kemp, E.B., 3rd (1992), Land loss rates: Louisiana coastal plain. Technical Report G1-92-2, USACE District, New Orleans.

Gibbs, M.J. (1984), Economic analysis of sea level rise: methods and results. In: Barth, M.C., & Titus, J.G., (eds.), *Greenhouse Effect and Sea Level Rise,* 215-251.

Gornitz, V., Lebedeff, S., & Hansen, J. (1982), Global sea level trend in the past century. *Science,* 215: 1611-1614.

Hoffman, J.S., Keyes, D. & Titus, J.G. (1983), Projecting future sea level rise: methodology, estimates to the year 2100, and research needs. US EPA Technical Report No. 230-09-007.

Hoffman, J.S., Wells, J.B., & Titus, J.G. (1986), Future global warming and sea level rise. In: Sigbjarnarson, F. (ed.), *Iceland Coastal and River Symposium,* National Energy Authority, Reykjavik.

Hull, C.H.J., & Titus, J.G. (eds.), (1986), *Greenhouse Effect, Sea Level Rise, and Salinity in the Delaware Estuary,* EPA Technical Report No. 230-05-86-010.

Kana, T.M., Michel, J., Hayes, M.O., & Jensen, J.R. (1984), The physical impact of sea level rise in the area of Charleston, South Carolina. In: Barth, M.C., & Titus, J.G. (eds.), *Greenhouse Effect and Sea Level Rise,* 105-150.

Keeling, C.D., Bacastow, R.B., & Whorf, T.P. (1982), Measurements of the concentration of carbon dioxide at Mauna Loa observatory, Hawaii. In: Clark. W., (ed.), *Carbon Dioxide Review,* Oxford University Press, New York, 377-384.

Leatherman, S.P. (1984), Coastal geomorphic responses to sea level rise: Galveston Bay, Texas. In: Barth, M.C., & Titus. J.G. (eds.), *Greenhouse Effect and Sea Level Rise,* 151-178.

McBride, R.A., Hiland, M.W., Penland, S., Williams, S.J., Byrnes, M.R., Westphal, K.A., Jaffe, B.E., & Sallenger, A.H., Jr. (1991), Mapping barrier island changes in Louisiana: techniques, accuracy and results. In: *Proceedings of the Coastal Sediments '91*, 1011-1026.

Meier, M.F. (ed.), (1985), *Glaciers, Ice Sheet and Sea Level*. National Academy Press, Washington, D.C.

Penland, S.,Ramsey, K.E., McBride, R.A., Moslow, T.F., & Westphal, K.A. (1989), Relative sea level rise and subsidence in Louisiana and the Gulf of Mexico. Coastal Geology Report No. 3, Louisiana Geological Survey.

Revelle, R. (1983), Probable future changes in sea level resulting from increased atmospheric carbon dioxide. In: *Changing Climate,* National Academic Press, Washington, D.C., 433-448.

Rotmans, J. (1990), *'IMAGE: An Integrated Assess of the Greenhouse Effect.* Kluwer Academic Publishers, Norwell, MA 02061.

Titus, J.G. (ed.), (1988), Greenhouse effect, sea level rise and coastal wetlands. EPA Technical Report, No. 230-05-86-013.

Chapter 8
Use of Mathematical Models in Policy Evaluation: Comments

Kathleen A. Miller

This volume presents an informative set of applications of mathematical models to environmental policy issues. The models described in these chapters range from highly detailed representations of production processes, tightly focused on assessing the effects of a particular policy proposal to less complicated models that capture enough detail on the interaction between an economic activity and environmental variables to provide useful estimates of policy impacts. The varying level of detail embodied in these models demonstrates the flexibility of mathematical approaches to the analysis of policy issues.

In general, this collection of papers suggests that rather simplified models can provide valuable insights regarding the effects of broad policy choices, while more complex models may be needed to sort out the effects of a specific policy, such as a ban on a particular herbicide, in a complex environment characterized by a multitude of technical options. Several of these chapters demonstrate that well-designed mathematical models of complex systems can illuminate important interlinkages between technological factors and economic decisions, allowing more reliable assessments of the nature and magnitude of the effects of particular policy options.

For example, Bouzaher and Shogren use an integrated system of process and behavioral models, the Comprehensive Environmental Economic Policy Evaluation System (CEEPES), to assess the impacts of two herbicide policies: 1) a ban on atrazine and 2) a ban on all triazines. Their evaluation includes impacts on net returns, acreages by crop and type of tillage, herbicide concentrations in surface and groundwater and human and aquatic vegetation exposure values. The purpose of their study is to present a comprehensive assessment of the effects of the policy options at the regional level. This requires the integration of detailed submodels of such factors as input substitution options for weed control together with their cost and effectiveness under varying weather conditions; the impact of weed competition on crop yields; farm-level economic decision making; leaching and chemical transport.

Because it would be prohibitively costly to run each possible policy option through the entire set of interlinked models and to perform adequate sensitivity analyses on the results, the authors employ a metamodeling approach. A metamodel is essentially a statistical model of the actual simulation model. Bouzaher and Shogren state that: "A key feature of the methodology is to statistically sample from micro data, calibrate and perform model simulations at the sampled points, and use statistical techniques to build parametric forms for prediction at the macro level." This allows them to abstract from the level of detail presented in the original environmental process and weed control input substitution models, translating them into a scale more appropriate to analysis of the effects of herbicide policies over a large region. Metamodeling thus allows models designed for the purpose of detailed analysis of the subcomponents of a complex system to be generalized and coupled with one another in a tractable representation of the entire system.

One of the benefits of this approach is that it highlights the fact that a realistic representation of the input substitution options is required to accurately assess the environmental and economic effects of a policy relating to one, or a small group of the weed control options available to farmers. Their work also lends support to the argument that agricultural policies should not be considered in isolation. Specifically, their CEEPES results enable them to demonstrate that the proposed bans on atrazine and triazines are likely to contribute to increased soil erosion by increasing the use of conventional tillage techniques. The increased erosion, in turn, contributes to higher herbicide concentrations in surface water.

The other chapter dealing with non-point source pollution, by Abler and Shortle, concentrates on more general questions. Their goal is to assess the effects of agricultural pricing reforms and direct restrictions on chemical inputs on the aggregate use of fertilizer and other agricultural chemicals in the United States and the European Community. Since estimation of actual changes in water quality or exposure values are not the goal of this chapter, there is no need to integrate environmental process models with the economic models as was done by Bouzaher and Shogren. Abler and Shortle are thus able to make use of a less complicated set of models for their analysis.

They develop two-level constant elasticity of substitution (CES) production functions for each of three commodities: wheat, coarse grains and soybeans. These are coupled with constant elasticity demand functions for the US and the EC and constant elasticity supply and demand functions for the rest of the world to estimate output, prices and trade flows for the three commodities. Impacts of specific policy scenarios on commodity, land and labor markets and on the use of fertilizer and other chemicals are estimated for the US and the EC.

Abler and Shortle note that the output elasticities derived from their models are much larger than econometric estimates of output elasticities for the same crops. They use this difference to argue that their own estimates should be interpreted as applying to the very long run, in which constraints imposed by the existing capital stock on input substitution disappear and are replaced by constraints only on available technical knowledge. They further argue that their model thus corresponds to "the concept of a metaproduction function, which can be regarded as the envelope of short-run production functions." They also derive short-run substitution elasticities from econometric supply elasticities.

Four policy scenarios are analyzed: 1) unilateral agricultural policy reforms in the EC, corresponding to the MacSharry Plan; 2) bilateral reforms involving adoption of the MacSharry Plan in the EC and 20% reductions in US support prices for wheat and coarse grains; 3) a 20% reduction in EC fertilizer use induced by taxes or other incentive mechanisms; and 4) a similarly induced 20% reduction in EC use of other chemicals. Their results suggest that unilateral MacSharry Plan reforms in the EC would substantially reduce the use of fertilizer and other chemicals in the EC, while increasing their use modestly in the US over the short term and substantially over the long term. Their analysis of bilateral reforms predicts environmental improvements in both regions, with potentially large reductions in fertilizer and chemical use over the long term. They further estimate that fertilizer restrictions in the EC would also reduce EC chemical use while slightly increasing US fertilizer and chemical applications and that the impacts of EC chemical restrictions would be similar but smaller in magnitude.

While Abler and Shortle argue that their results are qualitatively robust, they are careful to draw attention to the fact that the magnitudes of their impact estimates, particularly for the MacSharry Plan and bilateral commodity reforms, are subject to tremendous uncertainty. Their sensitivity analysis demonstrates that the estimated impacts of these policies are quite sensitive to the assumed values of the Allen elasticities of substitution. Given a paucity of available estimates of these elasticities for the EC and large disparities between estimates made in different studies for the US, they conclude that: "...EC policymakers are basically operating in the dark, while US policymakers are not too far ahead." While they find this result disappointing, it is significant in that it highlights a topic in need of further research and suggests that the payoff to improved estimates of these elasticities is potentially large.

Water pollution policy is also the focus of the chapter by Roan and Martin. That chapter develops a model of the effects of mining operations on water pollution downstream of the mine site arising from the leaching of minerals from mine waste piles. The model is quite simple, but it is adequate to provide useful approximations of the effects of more stringent water quality standards on the profitability of existing mining operations, on levels of mining and waste reclamation activity and on the minimum grade of ore that could profitably be developed by a new mine.

They apply the model to a hypothetical proposed open pit gold mine located in the Clearwater National Forest and estimate the effects of changes in the price of gold, the discount rate used by the mine manager and the water quality standard on the minimum ore grade that would have to be discovered to justify opening the mine. For example, they estimate that at $300/oz and a discount rate of 15% a regulation requiring stream metal concentrations to remain below 0.05 mg/L would require that the average ore grade exceed 0.089 oz/ton to justify opening the mine. In addition, they estimate the impact of more stringent water quality standards on the profitability of a hypothetical existing mine at the same location. In that example, discounted profits for a mine that has already discovered a deposit with an average ore grade of 0.04 oz/ton decrease from $6 million to slightly more than $2.5 million when the restriction on stream metal concentration is tightened from 0.1 milligrams per liter to 0.0 mg/L.

These results depend on characterizing the rate of metal migration to the stream as a constant function of the average rainfall at the proposed mine site. Stream metal concentrations thus depend on average rainfall, average streamflow and the size of the waste pile. One can imagine situations in which extreme rainfall events could have important temporary impacts on water quality, for example, if the rate of leaching sharply increased during heavy rainstorms. If such acute peaks could have long-term deleterious impacts on aquatic biota, then the analysis could be extended to consider the impact of restrictions on the frequency of such events on the maximum size of the waste pile and on mine profitability. The model presented here abstracts from such detailed considerations. It, thus, is geared toward analyzing cases where average metal concentration is the critical variable or where heavy rains can be assumed to provide enough additional streamflow so that concentrations would not fluctuate appreciably with rainfall variations.

The simplicity of this model would facilitate its use to explore a range of policy scenarios by altering assumptions regarding the metal price, the discount rate, mining and reclamation costs, the hydrological characteristics of the proposed mine site and the water quality standard. While the model does not capture all of the details of mining operations or of the impacts of metal concentrations on the stream environment, it can nevertheless be a useful tool for evaluating choices regarding water quality standards.

The chapter by Considine, Davis and Marakovits employs an engineering-economic model of the steel production process, specified as a linear programming problem. They couple this with a model of cancer incidence as a function of coke oven emissions to estimate the effects of two alternative environmental standards on total variable costs, employment, energy and materials use, capital expenditures and annual cancer cases. The policies examined are the MACT (Maximum Achievable Control Technology) standards proposed for 1995 and the tougher LAER (Lowest Achievable Emission Rate) standards scheduled for implementation in 1998.

The process model presented in this chapter incorporates a detailed depiction of the multiple operations in the steel production process along with technical alternatives for each processing operation. This allows the authors to identify the full range of input substitution possibilities and investment options available to steel producers seeking to minimize the cost of complying with the stricter environmental standards for coke oven emissions.

This highly informative process model allows the authors to demonstrate that when investment in new technology and changes in the level of coke imports are incorporated in the model, the estimated costs of meeting the standards are substantial lower than when compliance costs are estimated without allowance for such adjustments. Their estimates nevertheless demonstrate that, over a wide range of assumptions regarding the relationship between cancer risk and emissions, the cost of the proposed standards per avoided cancer case is rather high. Their estimates range from $10 - $30 million per annual cancer avoided for the MACT standards and from $21 - $57 million for the LAER standards.

This volume contains two chapters relating to facets of the problem of carbon dioxide accumulation and resulting global warming. The chapter by Haurie and Loulou examines alternative approaches to analyzing policy problems relating to the energy sector. Their survey emphasizes applications addressing the regional costs of reducing CO_2 emissions. The chapter by Curiel, Filar and Zapert assesses the possible relative magnitude of the contribution of global warming to coastal inundation in Louisiana.

Haurie and Loulou argue that mathematical programming systems analytic models can provide valuable insights on the economic effects of energy policies. They outline several examples of such applications, including analyses of policies aimed at reducing emissions of CO_2. They note that different types of models have different relative strengths, and they lay out criteria for evaluating the usefulness of alternate modeling approaches. Their criteria are as follows: I) a sufficiently detailed representation of the fundamental techno-economic options, ii) a coherent representation of the economic processes underlying the energy use, iii) good tractability of the simulations or scenario generator.

One of the models discussed in their chapter is a linear programming model of the energy supply sector (MARKAL) in which total costs of using an array of technologies to produce energy services are minimized, subject to satisfaction of exogenously given demands. In this model, the energy sector produces "energy carriers" which are further transformed into final energy services, the demands for which are specified as fixed and invariant with respect to price. Haurie and Loulou find that this model is sufficient to demonstrate that there would be large differences between adjacent Canadian provinces in the cost of meeting given targets for reducing CO_2 emissions.

They go on to examine cases in which final energy demands are specified according to an explicit demand law, or alternatively, in which local approximations of implicit demand functions are derived through sensitivity analysis performed on a linear programming consumption submodel. They find that the latter approach allows highly detailed, economically coherent models to be considered, but at the cost of some loss of tractability.

They next examine applications of mathematical programming in the context of imperfect competition. The effects of the PURPA regulation requiring utilities to buy electricity from cogenerators at the utility's marginal cost are examined for New England using a Nash equilibrium model. A Stackleberg price leader/price follower problem is formulated as a bi-level programming problem to examine the implications of price setting versus a cooperative solution for the Quebec electric power market over a 20 year horizon. The authors argue that such applications "add considerably to the set of economic situations that can be modeled formally." They note, however, that reliable, general algorithms do not exist for the computation of Nash and Stackelberg equilibria when the players are represented by large mathematical programs. A particular problem for the Stackleberg formulation is the risk of obtaining a local rather than a global solution.

Haurie and Loulou outline other applications, including an analysis of the gains from cooperative integration of the electric power systems of Quebec, Ontario, New England and New York. Their analysis incorporates a specification of the fair sharing of the gains from cooperation and they present estimates of optimal transmission line capacities required to implement the cooperative solution. Another application involves estimates of the benefits of electricity trading versus emissions rights trading under CO_2 emissions constraints for Ontario and Quebec. They conclude that decomposition techniques can improve the tractability of such problems and reduce computation costs.

Haurie and Loulou also devote considerable attention to the potential contributions of dynamic and stochastic programming methods to problems of risk management under uncertainty. They briefly discuss the applicability of a "parameter design" problem approach in cases where past decisions affect the probability distributions of the parameters of the programming model, and note that stochastic programming can be used where these probabilities are independent of past decisions. The stochastic programming approach makes use of an event tree to generate scenarios, each characterized by a given probability of occurrence. The optimization problem might be specified as minimizing expected cost over this set of scenarios. The authors describe a scenario aggregation approach to solving such stochastic programming problems, and discuss applications involving specification of tradeoffs between system costs and risk.

Haurie and Loulou's descriptions of these various applications of mathematical programming are brief and are written in a style accessible only to individuals well versed in mathematics. Nevertheless, this chapter can provide even non-specialists with a sense of the potential range of applications of mathematical programming models to energy policy issues.

The chapter by Curiel, Filar and Zapert combines outputs from the Dutch Integrated Greenhouse model, IMAGE, with local studies of coastal changes to estimate the relative importance of enhanced global warming on the Louisiana coastline. This chapter addresses the question of whether or not global warming would significantly accelerate the loss of coastal lands in Louisiana, given the rapid coastal changes already underway as a result of local geophysical processes. The extent to which coastal inundation can be slowed by policies aimed at controlling emissions of greenhouse gases is also addressed.

The authors focus their analysis on Eastern Terrebonne Parish, where the most comprehensive data are available. Linear models are developed to relate sea level rise, defined as consisting of a local component arising from local processes and a global component arising from the greenhouse effect, to changes in several coastline variables. These include shoreline retreat at specific locations and changes in total area for islands, marshes and portions of the coastal plain. In some cases, these variables are also estimated to depend on a time trend independent of sea level. The authors then compute the relative contribution of global warming, under alternate emissions scenarios, to changes in each of these variables. They find that sea level rise caused by global warming is likely to account for a relatively small portion of the land losses and related coastal changes in Louisiana up to the year 2100.

They note that estimates of error bounds for the impacts of sea level rise are only available for some of the coastal-change variables. Error estimates are also not yet available for the IMAGE outputs. Lacking this information, the authors chose not to conduct a sensitivity analysis of their results. However, where estimates of error bounds are reported, their range suggests that the conclusions of this study regarding future coastal changes could be quite sensitive to uncertainties surrounding the rates of local change.

The chapters in this volume present a wide range of techniques that can be applied to the analysis of environmental policy issues. While each paper is in some respects unique, each contributes to a coherent picture of how models can be tailored to address different policy-related questions. They suggest, for example, that it is appropriate to incorporate different degrees of complexity in a model depending upon the specificity of the question being addressed and the nature of the systems involved. Thus, questions like: "How would more stringent water quality standards affect the profitability of existing mining operations and the minimum ore grade that can be developed profitably by new mines?" can usefully be addressed with a very streamlined model of the type described by Roan and Martin. On the other hand, if the question is: "How much will it cost to reduce cancer incidence by implementing one or another specific policy applying to coke oven emissions?", then one would need a considerably more detailed model, coupled with highly accurate parameter estimates and reliable forecasts of the values of key variables.

In general, formal modeling is valuable to the extent that it assists systematic analysis of a complex decision problem by stripping away extraneous detail and focusing attention on the most important causal relationships and feedbacks. By their nature, models are simplifications of reality. If a model captures the interactions among key variables in a manner that adequately mimics reality, it can be a powerful predictive tool. However, there are always uncertainties surrounding model specification, both in the selection of variables to be included and in the selection of functional forms to describe relationships. In addition, estimation of parameter values and projections of the future values of important explanatory variables entail additional uncertainties. As a result of these various sources of potential error, models are imperfect tools. They can nevertheless be useful tools if the nature of the attendant uncertainties are properly understood and if the models are used as an aid in building an understanding of the potential range of outcomes of a policy choice rather than as simple "answer machines."

Models vary in their reliability, in that the range of forecasting error may be large or small. Forecasting error depends upon the goodness-of-fit and bias in parameter estimates and the sensitivity of results to underlying assumptions. Sensitivity analyses are important in policy applications because they give modelers and users a sense of the reliability of the model.

Reliability, however, is not the only criterion important in policy applications. The practical usefulness of a model for policy analysis depends not only upon the accuracy with which it reproduces the modeled relationships but also upon: 1) the degree to which the modeled variables are in fact observable and measurable in the real world, 2) the extent to which the model relates in a meaningful way to policy "handles" actually available to the policy makers, and 3) the degree to which the model encompasses the factors likely to be important in real-world decision making.

There may be tradeoffs between the reliability of a model and its complexity, as well as between complexity and usefulness. As demonstrated by several of the chapters in this volume, highly detailed models may be needed in cases where it is important to accurately represent complicated interactions between physical and economic subsystems. Relatively complex models are also needed in cases where decisions made by individuals operating in different spheres interact indirectly with one another, as exemplified by Abler and Shortle's analysis of the effects of an international commodities market on producers' decisions regarding pesticide and fertilizer applications. In such cases, simple models coupled with intuition are not sufficient to accurately forecast the effects of a policy change. However, as models become more complex, errors in specification, in parameter estimates or in the projected values of independent variables tend to become compounded and it becomes increasingly difficult to verify the model's accuracy. While a complex model can yield detailed answers, there is no guarantee that those answers are reliable. As for the usefulness of complex models, detailed results are sometimes necessary, but there may be instances in which the policy-maker would be better served by less detailed, but more accurate outputs.

Thus, model users need to be properly apprised of the nature and sources of uncertainty associated with the model, and their implications for its proper use. In some cases, a model may have its greatest usefulness as an interactive vehicle for exploring the policy terrain rather than as a source of defensible numerical estimates of the net benefits of a particular policy choice. The usefulness of a model can be enhanced by increasing its accessibility to the policy makers. A model is less likely to be treated as an unbelievable black-box if its structure is clearly evident and if the users understand and have confidence in its underlying assumptions. Hands-on experience with a user-friendly model can increase a policy-maker's confidence in a model, but unless the user is given an adequate understanding of what is going on inside of the model and the extent to which the outputs hinge upon initial assumptions and the accuracy of input data, that confidence may be misplaced.

A note of caution needs to be inserted here about use of the term "policy-maker." Policy-making is, in fact, frequently a contentious process that may involve legislative bodies, public agencies, the courts and representatives of multiple interests with a stake in the outcome of the policy process. While a single agency may have the authority to issue the regulation that the modeler is charged with analyzing, there frequently are other parties interested in influencing the policy choice. Such parties are likely to want access to any model used by a public agency in its policy analyses. Thus, making a model accessible and user-friendly in the interest of enhancing its proper use by public servants, may also encourage its use by a variety of other individuals with competing interests. In some cases, these parties may desire an honest evaluation of the impacts of the proposed change on their own interests, but they will also attempt to either use the model directly or to construct a plausible competing model to make as strong a case as possible for their own position in the policy debate.

The resulting "dueling model" phenomenon is not entirely unhealthy. When competing models are subjected to the intense scrutiny of regulatory hearings or court review, those with glaring weaknesses are weeded out. In addition, if a model does not produce reliable forecasts because its outputs are highly sensitive to minor differences in assumptions or to a plausible range of data errors, it is unlikely to survive the process of comparative assessment. One might suppose that, in an ideal world, the most accurate model (i.e., the one that can most accurately predict the real-world processes of concern) would win out. However, in a policy environment characterized by conflicting interests, it is the most convincing model that is likely to exert the greatest influence on the policy choice. In such circumstances, a correctly specified, objectively computed but poorly communicated model could be rejected in favor of a well-sold but strategically designed and, thus, inaccurate competitor.

Communication is thus central to ensuring that a model is evaluated on its merits in the policy forum. Effective communication between modelers and the policy community requires a common language. Although the language of mathematics is precise and clearly understandable to the initiated, it can be daunting even to well-educated professionals if they have not been trained in the particular mathematical technique being used. Clear explanation of purposes, assumptions, and methods is an important part of model presentation. Where the use of specialized terminology cannot be avoided, definitions appropriate to the intended audience should be included.

Some of the chapters in this volume do a better job of communicating the essence of the model, its purposes, derivation and outputs to non-specialists than others. In fact, it is not clear that all of these chapters were written with the same audience in mind. Some of the chapters appear to be aimed at a general, well-educated audience of policy professionals, while others are written in a style that would be more appropriate for a disciplinary journal. For example, while it is quite long and involved, the chapter by Considine *et al.* presents the model in clear English and defines most of the specialized terminology that is used. Their discussion of the purposes and strengths of their model and the uncertainties associated with their results is relatively easy for a non-specialist to read and follow. On the other hand, non-modelers would find the chapter by Haurie and Loulou rather difficult to understand given its cursory model descriptions presented with considerable use of a highly specialized vocabulary.

Skepticism regarding the usefulness of formal modeling is rather widespread in the policy community. To some extent, this results from poor communication or reactions to casual observations of the "dueling model" phenomenon. However, skepticism also arises from a well-founded sense of the limitations of formal models.

In many cases, factors that are difficult to measure or model nevertheless have an important bearing on the desirability of a particular policy option. Where this is the case, suspicions naturally arise regarding the validity of any formal model that ignores these factors. In fact, the policy prescriptions that would be produced by such a model -- solely by itself, are not likely to be socially optimal. However, if one does attempt to directly incorporate in the model such difficult-to-handle phenomena as cultural values, ethics, aesthetics, social equity or risk perceptions that differ markedly from measurable risks, there is no guarantee that the new "bottom-line" will have any greater validity or that it will point to a more socially optimal policy prescription. A better approach, perhaps, would be for modelers to openly and carefully acknowledge the limitations of the model and to constructively contribute to defining the proper place of the model in the overall policy context. If important, but difficult-to-handle factors are not incorporated in the model, the modeler should be prepared to clearly communicate that fact and to communicate why they are not included, and how their inclusion might affect not only the model's outputs but also the reliability of those outputs. In addition, the modeler should communicate a sense of how the model, with its acknowledged limitations, can nevertheless be useful in an overall policy analysis that incorporates broader considerations.

In general, this last step of describing the proper place of the model within the broader policy context is not something that comes naturally to the modeler. It is often easier to describe the result of optimization within the model as "the optimum" without going back to alert readers to the fact that the true social optimum may be different and may depend on factors outside of the model. Some of the chapters in this volume could be strengthened by devoting greater attention to this issue. For example, the chapter by Haurie and Loulou outlines a model of the gains from cooperative generation and transmission in the Northeast power market in which the "optimal" solution is characterized by greatly increased transmission capacity. However, no discussion is presented of the environmental or health concerns that might pertain to such an expansion of capacity and their possible implications for the optimal policy choice. While it might not be possible to directly incorporate such considerations in the model, it would be a simple matter to clearly state that the model, as constructed, provides a benchmark estimate of benefits against which environmental, health and aesthetic considerations can be compared.

At present, a backlash is evident in political circles against the application of scientific and mathematical approaches to policy issues. This has been fueled by the fall of Communism and perceptions that its failure was ultimately a failure of science-based planning. As Vaclav Havel put it:

> The modern era has been dominated by the culminating belief, expressed in different forms, that the world -- and Being as such -- is a wholly knowable system governed by a finite number of universal laws that man can grasp and rationally direct for his own benefit. ...
>
> Communism was the perverse extreme of this trend. It was an attempt, on the basis of a few propositions masquerading as the only scientific truth, to organize all of life according to a single model, and to subject it to central planning and control regardless of whether or not that was what life wanted.
>
> The fall of Communism can be regarded as a sign that modern thought -- based on the premise that the world is objectively knowable, and that the knowledge so obtained can be absolutely generalized -- has come to a final crisis.[1]

U.S. Congressman George Brown has drawn on Havel's insights in building his own critique of the role of science in society.[2] The Congressman's misgivings pertain primarily to the big physical science initiatives that have received substantial federal support, rather than to the type of policy-oriented models presented in this book. However, modelers would do well to take note of the sentiments upon which his criticisms are based. In essence, the Congressman charges that scientists have failed to come through on their implied promises to better the lot of the average citizen. One could argue that this charge is based on misunderstandings -- either of promises made, progress achieved or of the actual causes of the relative economic decline of the U.S. middle-class. But whether the Congressman's position is based on valid criticism or misunderstanding, it should alert modelers to the fact that they will need to pay greater attention in the future to justifying the usefulness of their models and to demonstrating the ways in which the proper use of models can, in fact, promote human welfare.

---

[1]Vaclav Havel, "The End of the Modern Era," *The New York Times.* March 1, 1992.

[2]George E. Brown, Jr., "The Objectivity Crisis," *American Journal of Physics* 60 (September, 1992): 779-781; George E. Brown, Jr., "Global Change and the New Definition of Progress," *Geotimes* (June, 1992): 19-21.

Index

AAtrex, *see* Atrazine
Accent (nicosulfuron), 23, 24–25, 28, 29, 30, 32, 33, 36, 37, 38, 39
Admissible perfect foresight strategy, 151
Agricultural Land Management Alternatives with Numerical Assessment Criteria (ALMANAC), 13, 14, 16, 17
Alachlor, *see* Lasso
Allen elasticities of substitution (AES), 46, 51–52, 70
ALMANAC, *see* Agricultural Land Management Alternatives with Numerical Assessment Criteria
American Iron and Steel Institute (AISI), 106, 107–110
Antarctica, 162, 164, 165
Aquatic vegetation, 36–38
Atrazine ban, 8, 38–40
  acute exposure values for surface water, 28–33
  CEEPES on, 17, 20, 22–24, 185–186
  chronic exposure levels for groundwater, 30
  economic indicators and, 24–28
  environmental indicators and, 28
  exposure values for aquatic vegetation, 36–38
  exposure variability and, 33–36
Auxiliary perfect foresight problems, 152

Bang-bang solution, 83, 86
Banvel (dicamba), 23, 29, 30, 31, 32, 33–36, 37, 38, 39
Basagran (bentazon), 23, 29, 30, 31, 32, 37, 39
Bayou LaFourche, 167
Beacon (primisulfuron), 20, 23, 24–25, 28, 29, 30, 32, 33, 36, 37, 38, 39, 40
Beehive coke ovens, 106
Bentazon, *see* Basagran
Benzene soluble organics (BSOs), 103, 106, 109, 110, 112
Bilateral reforms, 61–64, 187
Bi-level programming problem, 136–137
Bladex (cyanazine), 8, 20, 23, 28, 29, 30, 31, 32, 33, 34, 35, 37, 39
Blast furnaces, 109, 113
BLAYER, 16, 19
Bromoxynil, *see* Buctril
Brown, George, 197
Buctril (bromoxynil), 23, 29, 30, 32, 37, 39

Bureau of Mines, U.S., 80, 83, 91
Butylate, *see* Sutan

Cancer, 103, 109–110, 112, 114, 120–121, 189
Carbon dioxide emissions, 189–191
  enhanced greenhouse effect and, 163–164, 165
  marginal costs of abatement, 127–130
  trading rights for, 141–144, 145, 146, 191
CEEPES, *see* Comprehensive Environmental Economic Policy Evaluation System
Chandeleur Islands, 167
Charleston, South Carolina, 162
Clean Air Act Amendments, 4, 103, 106
Clean Water Act (CWA), 3–4, 77–100, *see also* Ecosystem constraint modeling
Clearwater National Forest, 91–95, 188
Coarse grains, *see* Environment & trade policy linkage modeling
Cobb-Douglas functions, 45
Co-generators, 135–136
Coke imports, 110, 113, 114
Coke oven emission controls, 4, 103–121, 189
  door leakage and, 106, 109–110, 120
  five options for complying with, 105–106
  input parameter distributions in, 110–112
  process model in, 107–110, 121
  stochastic sensitivity analysis of, 110, 112–121
  technology and, 104–107
Column generation techniques, 154
Commodity policy reforms, 54–56
Common Agricultural Policy (CAP), 3, 44, 45, 55, 61, 71
Comprehensive Environmental Economic Policy Evaluation System (CEEPES), 3, 7–8, 16, 38, 185–186
  application of, 22–24
  experimental design of, 17
  integration of, 20
Constant elasticity of substitution, *see* Two-level constant elasticity of substitution
Consumer subsidy equivalents (CSE), 53
Conventional tillage, 25–28, 30, 31, 33, 38, 186

Cooperation dividends, 139–140
Cooperative optimum, 135
Corex process, 107, 109, 111, 113, 114,
    120
Corn, 16, 22–24, 28, 29
Corn Belt, 15, 22, 24, 25, 26, 27, 28, 29,
    30, 31, 33, 38
Cournot-Nash equilibria, 155
Curse of dimensionality, 148
Cyanazine, *see* Bladex

2,4–D, 23, 28, 29, 30, 32, 35, 36, 37, 38,
    39
Decision analysis problems, 155
Decision in uncertainty paradigm, 124
Decomposition techniques, *see*
    Supply-demand decomposition
    techniques
Delaware estuary, 163
Demand
    for coke, 114, 115, 118
    in environment & trade policy linkage
        modeling, 48, 53
    in equilibria & risk modeling, 124, 131,
        134–135
Department of Agriculture, U.S. (USDA),
    3, 7, 8–9, 25
Department of Energy, U.S., 107
Dicamba, *see* Banvel
Direct reduction, 107
Dual (metolachlor), 23, 29, 30, 31, 32, 33,
    35, 36, 37, 39
Dueling model phenomenon, 194–195
Dulac, 168, 176
Dynamic programming approach,
    147–149, 191

Early retirement programs, 56, 71
Eastern Terrebonne Parish, 166, 168, 191
Ecosystem constraint modeling, 3–4,
    77–100, 188–189
    case study of, 91–95
    description of model, 78–82
    linear cost functions in, 83–91
    state-space boundary in, 86, 99–100
Electricity trading, 141–144, 145, 191
Emission rights trading, 141–144, 145,
    146, 191
Emission taxes, 126
Energy exports, 125
Energy imports, 125
Energy production model, 124–126
Energy supply function, 124–126
Engineering-economic model, 104, 189

Enhanced greenhouse effect, 5, 161–181,
    191–192
    background on, 162–163
    description of area and variables,
        166–168
    description of model, 168–171
    IMAGE and, *see* Integrated Model to
        Assess the Greenhouse Effect
    methodology and results of study,
        165–166
    numerical results of scenario
        simulations, 179–181
Environmental policy reforms, 56–57
Environmental Protection Agency (EPA)
    coke oven emission controls and, 4,
        105, 106, 110, 114
    ecosystem constraints and, 77
    enhanced greenhouse effect and, 163
    nonpoint source pollution and, 3, 7,
        8–9, 22, 23, 25, 28, 33
Environmental Quality Management, Inc.,
    106
Environment & trade policy linkage
    modeling, 3, 43–71, 186–187
    agricultural policy and, 48–49, 53
    bilateral reforms in, 61–64, 187
    commodity policy reforms in, 54–56
    description of model, 45–50
    environmental policy reforms in, 56–57
    MacSharry plan in, 54–56, 58–61, 67,
        70, 71, 187
    parameter values and data sources in,
        50–54
    reduction of chemicals in, 67, 69
    reduction of fertilizers in, 64–67, 68
    sensitivity analysis in, 70
EPTC, *see* Eradicane
Equilibria & risk modeling, 4–5,
    123–156, 189–191
    emission rights trading in, 141–144,
        145, 146, 191
    energy supply function in, 124–126
    fair sharing of cooperation dividends
        in, 139–140
    final energy forms in, *see* Final energy
        forms
    game theory in, *see* Game theory
    MARKAL in, *see* MARKAL
    risk management in, 146–155
Eradicane (EPTC), 23, 29, 37
ETSAP, 127, 155
European Union (EU), *see* Environment
    & trade policy linkage modeling
Event trees, 149–150, 191

Executive Order 12866, 97
Export subsidies (restitutions), 49

Fate and Transport models, 15
Federal Food, Drug, and Cosmetic Act
    (FFDCA), 8
Federal Insecticide, Fungicide, and
    Rodenticide Act (FIFRA), 8
Feedback laws, 148
Fertilizers, see Environment & trade
    policy linkage modeling
Final energy forms, 126–127
    explicit demand for, 130–132
    implicit demand for, 132–133
Food, Agricultural, Conservation, and
    Trade Act, 9
Food Security Act, 9
France, 51

Galveston Bay, Texas, 162
Game theory, 123, 134, see also Nash
    equilibria; Stackelberg equilibria
General Agreement on Tariffs and Trade
    (GATT), 2, 43–44, 55, 56
Global environmental constraints,
    modeling under, see Equilibria &
    risk modeling
Global warming, see Enhanced
    greenhouse effect
Glyphosate, see Roundup
Gramaxine, see Paraquat
Greenhouse effect
    enhanced, see Enhanced greenhouse
        effect
    relative, 169–170, 175
Greenhouse gases, 163, 174
Greenhouse insurance, 155
Greenland, 162, 164, 165
Groundwater, nonpoint source pollution
    and, 28, 30

Havel, Vaclav, 197
HEAPREC, 92
Houma Tide gage station, 166, 168, 169,
    173, 174
Hydropower generation, risk assessment
    in, 154–155

Illinois, 33–36
IMAGE, see Integrated Model to Assess
    the Greenhouse Effect
Implementable strategies, 152, 154
Imports
    coke, 110, 113, 114

energy, 125
Industrial Source Complex Model,
    109–110
Inelastic energy service demands, 126–130
Input substitution, 9–13
Integrated mills, 108–109
Integrated Model to Assess the
    Greenhouse Effect (IMAGE),
    161–162, 169, 173, 191–192
    description of, 164–165
    SEAL and, 177–178
Interior point algorithms, 154
Intervention prices, 49
Iowa, 24, 33–36
Ireland, 52
Isles Dernieres, 167

Jewell version of non-recovery coke oven,
    106, 111, 113, 114, 120

LAER, see Lowest Achievable Emission
    Rate
Lake Felicity, 168
Lake States, 22, 24, 25, 31, 38
Lasso (alachlor), 23, 29, 30, 31, 32, 33,
    34, 35, 36, 37, 39
Latin Hypercube sampling, 112
Life of mines, 97–98
Linear cost functions, 83–91
Linear programming (LP) models
    of coke oven emission controls, 108,
        112–113, 189
    of equilibria & risk, 125, 127, 135, 141
    of nonpoint source pollution, 16
Lolo Creek, 91
Louisiana, coastal changes in, see
    Enhanced greenhouse effect
Lowest Achievable Emission Rate
    (LAER), 4, 105, 110, 112, 113,
    120–121, 189
    comparison of base case and, 119–120
    estimated average coke market
        adjustments under, 118

MacSharry Plan, 54–56, 58–61, 67, 70,
    71, 187
MACT, see Maximum Achievable
    Control Technology
Marginal costs, 84, 124, 132
    of carbon dioxide emission abatement,
        127–130
    utility purchase from co-generators at,
        135
Marginal revenue, 84

MARKAL, 5, 127–128, 130, 132, 141,
    155, 190
  feedback laws for, 148
Market allocation, 126–130, *see also*
    MARKAL
Market-clearing identities, 50
Market equilibrium paradigm, 123
Marshes, 168
Maximum Achievable Control
    Technology (MACT), 4, 105, 110,
    112, 113, 114, 120, 189
  comparison of base case and, 116–117
  estimated average coke market
    adjustments under, 115
MEDEQ, 132
Metal migration, 80, 86, 92
Metamodels, 3, 13–22, 185–186
  defined, 7
  functions of, 14
  role in estimate of environmental
    consequences, 15
  role in integration, 16
Metolachlor, *see* Dual
Mini-mills, 108–109
Mining, 3–4, 77–100, 188–189, *see also*
    Ecosystem constraint modeling
Mining waste piles, 79, 80–81, 86–87,
    89–91, 92, 97, 188
Mining waste reclamation, 80–81, 82, 84,
    89, 92, 97, 99, 188
Missouri, 24, 33–36
Model integration, 16–22
MUSS, 130

Nash equilibria, 134–136, 139, 190
National Emission Standards for
    Hazardous Air Pollutants
    (NESHAP), 105
Natural gas, 112
Netherlands, 165
New England, 5, 135, 140–141, 142, 143,
    190, 191
New York, 140–141, 142, 143, 191
Nicosulfuron, *see* Accent
Nonpoint source pollution modeling, 2–3,
    7–40, 185–186
  acute exposure values for surface
    water, 28–33
  CEEPES, *see* Comprehensive
    Environmental Economic Policy
    Evaluation System
  chronic exposure levels for
    groundwater, 28, 30
  economic indicators and, 24–28

environmental indicators and, 28
  exposure values for aquatic vegetation,
    36–38
  exposure variability and, 33–36
  input substitution and, 9–13
  integration in, 16–22
  metamodels in, *see* Metamodels
Northern Plains, 22, 24, 25, 31, 33

Off-gases, coke, 108, 109, 112
Ontario, 5, 127–130, 140–144, 146, 191
Optimal control theory, 4
  bang-bang solution in, 83, 86
Ore extraction, 79, 81–82, 84, 89, 92
Organization for Economic Cooperation
    and Development (OECD), 127, 156

PAL, 16, 19
Paraquat (Gramaxine), 23, 37
Pendimethalin, *see* Prowl
Pendimethel, 37
Perfect foresight strategy, 150–151
  admissible, 151
  auxiliary problems in, 152
Pesticide Root Zone Model (PRZM), 15,
    19
Pesticides, *see* Environment & trade
    policy linkage modeling; Nonpoint
    source pollution modeling
PIES model, 131–132
Plaquemines, 167
Price setters, 136
Price takers, 136
Primisulfuron, *see* Beacon
Princep (simazine), 8, 23, 28, 29, 30, 31,
    32, 33, 34, 35, 37, 39
Process models, 107–110, 121
Producer subsidy equivalents (PSE), 53
Propachlor, *see* Ramrod
Prowl (pendimethalin), 23, 28, 29, 30, 32,
    39
PRZM, *see* Pesticide Root Zone Model
Pulverized coal injection (PCI)
    technology, 107
PURPA rule, 135–136, 190

Quebec, 5, 127–130, 132–133, 137,
    140–144, 146, 190, 191

RACT, *see* Reasonably Available Control
    Technology
Rainfall, 80, 86, 91–92, 188
Ramrod (propachlor), 23, 29, 30, 32, 37,
    39

RAMS, *see* Resource Adjustable
    Modeling System
Random scenarios, 147
Reasonably Available Control
    Technology (RACT), 105
Relative greenhouse effect, 169–170, 175
Relaxed double schedules, 131
Resource Adjustable Modeling System
    (RAMS), 16, 17, 18, 20, 24
Restitutions (export subsidies), 49
Risk management, 146–155
Risk of the Unsaturated/Saturated
    Transport and Transformation of
    Chemical Concentration (RUSTIC),
    15, 16, 17, 18, 19
Roundup (glyphosate), 23, 28, 29, 37
RUSTIC, *see* Risk of the
    Unsaturated/Saturated Transport and
    Transformation of Chemical
    Concentration

S-adapted strategies, 155
SAFTMOD, 15, 19
Scenario aggregation, 149–150, 152
Scenarios, 149–154
    defined, 149
    random, 147
Scrap-based steelmaking, 107
SEAL, 177–178
Sea level rise, 162–164, 173, 174, 192
    model of, 168–171
    SEAL and, 177–178
    seven factors in, 166–167
Sensitivity analysis
    in environment & trade policy linkage
        modeling, 70
    in equilibria & risk modeling, 132
    stochastic, 110, 112–121
Shadow prices
    in ecosystem constraints modeling, 82,
        84
    in environment & trade policy linkage
        modeling, 47
    in equilibria & risk modeling, 124, 126
Shapley values, 140–141, 142, 144
Simazine, *see* Princep
Single optimization equilibrium model,
    126–127
Sodium silicate luting compounds, 4, 106
Soil erosion, 9, 25–28, 186
Sorghum, 16, 22–24, 28, 31, 33
Soybeans

environment & trade policy linkage
    and, *see* Environment & trade
    policy linkage modeling
nonpoint source pollution and, 25
Stackelberg equilibria, 136–138, 139, 190
State-space boundary, 86, 99–100
Status quo, 135–136, 141, 142, 143
Stochastic programming approach,
    149–154, 191
Stochastic sensitivity analysis, 110,
    112–121
STREAM, 16, 17, 19
Stream flow, 80, 91–92, 188
Supply
    of coke, 114, 115, 118
    in environment & trade policy linkage
        modeling, 44, 45–48, 50–53
    in equilibria & risk modeling, 124, 131,
        134–135
Supply-demand decomposition
    techniques, 132–134, 144–146
Supply-demand equilibrium paradigm,
    124, 127
Surface water, nonpoint source pollution
    and, 28–33
Sutan (butylate), 23, 29, 30, 32, 37, 39

Terrebonne Bay, 168
Thompson non-recovery coke oven,
    Jewell version, *see* Jewell version of
    non-recovery coke oven
Threshold prices, 49
Tillage, 22
    conventional, 25–28, 30, 31, 33, 38, 186
    reduced, 33
Timbalier Bay, 168
Timbalier Islands, 167, 174, 175
Triazine ban, 8, 38–40
    acute exposure values for surface
        water, 28–33
    CEEPES on, 17, 22–24, 185–186
    economic indicators and, 24–28
    environmental indicators and, 28
    exposure values for aquatic vegetation,
        36–38
    exposure variability and, 33–36
Two-level constant elasticity of
    substitution (CES), 45, 47, 186–187

Uruguay Round, 44
Utilities, 135–136

VADOFT, 15, 19
von Liebig response functions, 45

Waste, *see* Mining waste
Water quality, *see* Ecosystem constraint
    modeling; Environment & trade
    policy linkage modeling; Nonpoint
    source pollution modeling
Weather Impact Simulation on Herbicide
    (WISH), 10–13, 16, 17, 24
Wester Germany, 51–52

Wet coking process, 104, 112–113
Wheat, *see* Environment & trade policy
    linkage modeling
Wisconsin, 33–36
WISH, *see* Weather Impact Simulation on
    Herbicide

X2,4–D, *see* 2,4–D